To Cheryl

Enjoy

Vijay

A GUIDE TO AYURVEDIC COOKING

Vijay Jain, M.D.

Published by Family Cookbook Project, LLC
PO Box 475, South Wellfleet, MA 02663 (printed in Canada)

ISBN 978-1954262027

The Family Cookbook Project provided layout designs and graphical elements are copyright Family Cookbook Project, LLC, 2022. This book was created using the FamilyCookbookProject.com software app. The book author retains sole copyright to his or her contributions to this book.

Family Cookbook Project - Helping families collect cherished recipes forever. Visit us on the Web at www.familycookbookproject.com

D1478050

You can reach Dr. Jain at vijay@vijayjainmd.com
or through his website www.mindbodywellnessflorida.com

Dr. Vijay Jain, M.D.
Ayurvedic and Integrative Medicine Physician

Dr. Jain brings 40 years of experience in General Surgery and 23 years of focused study of Ayurvedic Medicine to his engaging integration of traditional/Western medicine with ancient Ayurveda. In addition to his Ayurveda practice, Dr. Jain teaches Ayurvedic certificate courses. He specializes in Ayurvedic Detoxification Panchakarma therapies and Rasayana (Tissue Tonifying) therapies for chronic lifestyle diseases and for graceful aging. Dr. Jain is co-author of the book entitled *"Unfolding Happiness"* based on the principles of Yoga and Ayurveda.

Denise Majewski

Denise met Dr. Jain as a participant in his Ayurvedic Panchakarma program. Intrigued with the Ayurvedic manner of cooking, she yearned to master its techniques. Serendipity stepped in when their intentions coincided: Denise learning this style of cooking and Dr. Jain compiling his recipes for those requesting them. Thus developed a partnership and friendship while creating this cookbook for you.

PRINCIPLES of AYURVEDIC COOKING AND EATING

"When nutrition is wrong, medicine is of no use.
When nutrition is right, medicine is of no need."
- Ayurvedic proverb

"Let Food by thy Medicine" is a guiding principle of Ayurveda. Ayurveda, the science of life, possesses ancient wisdom that gives us tools to live life to our fullest potential. We have the power to change our physical body by bringing in experiences through our senses of sight, sound, taste, smell, and touch. Ayurveda places a great deal of emphasis on nutrition, digestion, metabolism, and the sense of taste. Most of the imbalances in the body can be corrected by adjustments to nutrition and the intake of food and spices.

The body's digestive fire is called Agni. Agni is needed to digest anything we eat and it needs to be nurtured. All food is divided into **Six Tastes**, all of which are needed to create a balanced meal. These six tastes are sweet, sour, salty, pungent, bitter, and astringent. Having all six tastes in each meal means the meal is perfectly balanced to nurture your senses, relax your digestion, and harmonize feelings. In the back of this book is a questionnaire to assist in determinating your particular Dosha, or constitution, and whether you have an imbalance. Sweet, sour, and salty foods will balance Vata Dosha. Light sweet, bitter, and astringent foods balance Pitta Dosha. Kappa dosha is balanced by pungent, bitter, and astringent foods.

HOW YOU EAT: as important as what you eat so here are some helpful techniques

- Provide a calm environment, away from distractions like TV, phones, computers.
- Eat only when hungry. Eating when you're not hungry makes food harder to digest. Undigested food turns into toxins that deposit in tissues, creating obesity and other lifestyle diseases.
- Eat until you're 3/4 full, leaving room for food to churn, digest, and move through your system.
- Give thanks to the earth, sun, rain, and food for nurturing you and your body.

WHAT TO EAT: concentrate on fresh, home-cooked meals

- Start your day with a cup of warm water to aid digestion.
- Concentrate on eating non-GMO, organic, local, seasonal, and fresh foods.

WHEN TO EAT:

- Breakfast is best between 6-10 AM. This meal can be skipped if one is not hungry.
- Lunch is best between 10 AM-2 PM and should be the largest meal of the day.
- Dinner is best before 6 PM and should be smaller than lunch.

AVOID:

- Ice and ice-cold drinks.
- Leftovers: Storing, freezing, and microwaving food destroys nutritional value.
- Animal milk should not be combined with any other foods. It is okay to drink alone and with an hour between any other meal. Milk can be boiled and cooled to avoid indigestion. Non-dairy milk is also fine to drink.
- Mixing fruits: eat one specific fruit at a time, preferably late in the afternoon.
- Refined sugar, sweetened and prepared foods/snacks decrease energy and hinder digestion.

SIX TASTES FOR EVERY MEAL

This list is not complete but examples of what each meal should include.

1. Sweet: satisfies Vata and Pitta Doshas

Most grains (wheat, rice, barley, corn, most breads), most legumes (beans, lentils, peas), milk products (cream, butter, ghee), fruits (dates, grapes, pears, mangoes), cooked veggies (potatoes, sweet potatoes, carrots, beets), oils (ghee, olive, coconut, sesame, butter), nuts (almonds, walnuts, pistachios, nut milks and pastes), sunflower seeds, sugar in any form, honey

2. Sour: Vata satisfying

Fruits (lemon, lime, sour oranges), milk products (sour cream, whey, yogurt, cheese), fermented products (wine, vinegar, soy sauce, sour cabbage, pickles)

3. Salty: Vata satisfying

Any kind of salt or foods where large amounts of salt are added, seafood

4. Pungent: Kapha satisfying

Spices (chili, black pepper, mustard seeds, ginger, cumin, garlic, coriander, fennel, basil, dill), veggies (radish, onion)

5. Bitter: Pitta and Kapha pacifying

Fruits (olives, grapefruit), veggies (green & leafy, spinach, green cabbage, brussels sprouts, zucchini, eggplant, bitter gourd, chicory), chocolate, coffee, spices (turmeric, fenugreek)

6. Astringent: Pitta and Kapha pacifying

Veggies (beans, legumes, lentils), nuts (walnuts, hazelnuts, cashews), pumpkin seeds, honey, teas (black, green, white), veggies (sprouts, lettuce, green & leafy), rhubarb, most raw veggies, honey

HAVE FUN and be creative by mixing and matching one of each of these tastes into your meals to create delicious Ayurvedic dishes.

HOW TO USE THIS COOKBOOK

This cookbook has been designed to provide enough recipes for four weeks. Once you've mastered the art of Ayurvedic cooking, you'll find your favorite recipes and understand how to tweak them for your individual tastes in grains, greens, spices, and vegetables. Ayurvedic meals combine plant-based, local/seasonal, non-GMO, and organic foods into healthy, tasty meals.

First, take the questionnaire in the back so you understand if you are a Pitta, Vata, or Kapha dosha, or a combination of these. This will be important for notes at the bottom of the recipes. Tridoshic means the recipe is good for all 3 types of constitution. Next, see if you need additional equipment from the list below. Last, stock your pantry from the list of ingredients included. If you are not familiar with some of these ingredients, don't be wary of trying them. We've included a list of substitutions, as well. Once you have the pantry staples on hand, your weekly shopping list will be fresh produce and items needed for the recipes chosen. If a recipe includes a vegetable of which you are not fond, substitute a favorite one, no problem. Yes, this may be a different way of cooking than you are accustomed to, but you will be pleasantly surprised by the flavor of these recipes and the energy you will gain. Good luck and happy eating!

KITCHEN EQUIPMENT ESSENTIALS

Good, sharp knives

A pressure cooker or Instant Pot

Grater, handheld and/or microplaner

Large skillet or wok

Measuring cups and spoons

Vegetable peeler

Blender and/or handheld immersion blender

Coffee/spice grinder

These recipes have been collected from a variety of sources. We have modified them to follow Ayurvedic practice by ensuring all six tastes are present. Dr. Jain's notes at the bottom of the page are intended to aid individuals as to which recipes are best for them according to dosha.

Practice these recipes. Choose your favorites. HAVE FUN being creative with grains, greens, and vegetables used as medicine in Ayurvedic cooking.

PANTRY ITEMS (1 month of stock)

Olives: black or green olives, Kalamata
Dill pickle relish
Ketchup (no high fructose corn syrup)
Spicy Mustard
Low Sodium Soy Sauce (Bragg's)
Coconut Aminos
Vinegar: Apple Cider Vinegar, Balsamic, Red Wine, Rice
Coconut Milk
Unsweetened Applesauce
Beans: Black, Kidney, Garbanzo (chickpeas), Northern White, Cannellini, Pinto, Lima
Vegetable Broth, low sodium
Diced Tomatoes, with and without chilis
Tomato Sauce
Tomato Paste
Pasta Sauce, oil free, low sodium
Dried Lentils: red, green, brown
Sun Dried Tomatoes
Roasted Red Peppers, no oil
Salsa
Nut Butters (no oil added)

Whole Grains

Steel Cut Oats
Quinoa
Farro
Bulgar
Rice: Brown, Basmati, Jasmine, Black or Red, Wild
Whole Grain Pasta and Bean Flour Pasta
100% Whole Grain: Bread, Tortillas, Pasta, Pitas, Corn Tortillas
Flour: Whole Wheat, Almond, Chickpea, Oat

Nuts & Dried Fruits

Medjool Dates
Golden Raisins
Dried Cranberries, Cherries and Blueberries
Unsweetened Coconut Flakes
Nuts: Almonds (whole & sliced), Walnuts, Pecans, Brazil, Macadamia, Hazelnuts, Cashews, Pine, Pistachios

Seeds, Spices and Baking Products (3 months of stock)

Turmeric Powder
Ground Coriander & Coriander Seeds
Garam Masala
Fennel Seeds
Sesame Seeds
Italian Seasoning (with oregano, rosemary, basil, thyme, dill)
Nutmeg
Cinnamon
Black Peppercorns
Ginger Powder
Fenugreek seeds or powder
Garlic Powder
Onion Powder
Ground Cumin & Cumin Seeds
Celery seeds
Smoked Paprika
Cayenne Pepper
Vanilla Extract
Nutritional Yeast (not bakers yeast)
Unsweetened Cocoa Powder
Baking Powder
Baking Soda
Seeds: Sunflower, Pumpkin, Ground Flax, Chia
Hing (Asafetida)

Refrigerated Products (2 weeks of stock)

Organic soft, medium and extra firm tofu
Tempeh
Milks: Soy, Almond, Oat, Cashew, coconut
Non-Dairy Yogurt
Fresh Herbs: Cilantro, Parsley, Garlic, Basil, Rosemary, Ginger Root, Thyme, Fenugreek, Minced Garlic, Turmeric

---

Fruits and Vegetables

Use locally grown, seasonal, organic fruits and vegetables whenever possible.

SUBSTITUTIONS

Until your pantry is fully stocked with Ayurvedic cooking ingredients, you may need to substitute an item or two. Here are a few ideas for substituting basic ingredients in this cookbook. Whenever grains are in a recipe you can use what you have on hand, including rice, barley, farro, quinoa, bulgur, millet, oats, etc. If you want to substitute vegetables, go ahead, just be careful of how long each one takes to cook and adjust accordingly. The same holds true for the grains and greens. Greens can be substituted: kale vs spinach vs chard vs arugula vs collard vs cabbage. Use what you have and what you like. The same goes for fruit. There are recipes where we use certain spice mixes or sauces. We've included many of the recipes for these but if you can find healthy, organic, store bought ones without preservatives, use them (e.g. pasta sauce, hummus or masala spice mixes)

Anywhere we mention salt - use Himalayan salt or sea salt

Anywhere we mention black pepper - use freshly ground black pepper

Bread - multi-grain with seeds, Ezekiel, or unleavened bread

Soy sauce - use Amino Acids or tamari or coconut amino

Nut paste - use almond, cashew, hazelnut

Tahini - sesame seed paste

Protein - beans of any kind, tempeh or tofu

Eggs - Use an egg substitute; 1 whole egg is 1/4 c liquid egg substitute, or 1 tablespoon of flax meal plus 3 tablespoons water

Milk - use a non-dairy milk substitute such as soy, almond, cashew. Brands we like include Addjoi and Elmhurst because they don't include preservatives.

Oils - use coconut oil for cooking and extra virgin olive oil for dressings

Sweeteners - use maple syrup, agave, honey, dates, or raw sugar

Seeds - pumpkin, pepita, hemp, chia, sunflower, pomegranate, flax, sesame

Ground Flaxseed - flax meal

Ajwain or Carom Seeds - celery seeds

Table of Contents

BREAKFAST

Avocado Toast

2 pieces multi-grain bread
1 avocado
2 T hummus (Recipe in Dips, Dressings & Drinks)
Sea salt and black pepper to taste
1/4 teaspoon of garam masala
Handful of washed kale, spinach or arugula
Optional: sprouts, pumpkin seeds or walnuts

Toast bread. Spread hummus and ripe avocado slices onto toast. Top with greens and add any additional toppings.

Number of Servings: 1

Prep Time: 5 minutes

Personal Notes: A great way to break your fast for Vata and Pitta individuals.

Baked Fruit with Nuts (Tridoshic)

1 apple, cut in chunks
1 Asian pear, cut in chunks
1 tsp coconut oil
1/2 tsp chaat masala (Recipe in Sauces, Spice Mixes &
 Chutneys)
1/2 tsp cardamom
1/4 tsp cloves
1/4 tsp cinnamon
1/4 tsp black pepper
1/4 cup walnuts or pumpkin seeds

Preheat oven to 325°. Mix all ingredients in a bowl and place on a baking pan covered with brown parchment paper. Bake for 10 minutes. Serve warm.

Number of Servings: 4

Prep Time: 10 minutes

Chickpea Pancakes (Tridoshic)

Pancakes:
1 green onion, finely chopped
1/2 c chickpea flour (aka Besan or garbanzo flour)
1/4 tsp garlic powder
1/4 tsp Himalayan salt
1/8 tsp black pepper
1/4 tsp baking powder
1/2 tsp garam masala
1/4 tsp fenugreek powder
1/2 c and 2 T water
1 tsp coconut oil
Toppings: Salsa, avocado, hummus (Recipes in Dips, Dressings & Drinks)

Preheat skillet with coconut oil. Whisk together the flour and all the spices. Add the water and whisk until smooth. When the skillet is medium heat, pour in the batter and spread it out to make 2 large pancakes. Cook about 5 minutes on one side, until you can easily flip it. Cook another 5 minutes. These will take longer to cook than regular pancakes and will look browned. Serve this savory pancake with the toppings of your choice, such as hummus or salsa and avocado.

Number of Servings: 2

Prep Time: 15 minutes

Personal Notes: This recipe is great for brunch as they are heavy and filling.

Eggless Scramble with Tofu

4 oz soft tofu
1/2 c veggies of your choice; broccoli, onions etc.
1/4 c non dairy milk; e.g. Pure Cashew or Pure Almond
1 T Ghee
1/2 tsp garam masala
1 tsp nutritional yeast
1/2 tsp turmeric
1/2 tsp garlic powder
Sea salt and black pepper to taste

Place small cubes of tofu in a bowl. Mash the tofu until it looks scrambled. Heat Ghee in a skillet and sauté veggies for 3-4 minutes. Add all the spices. Add the tofu and cook another few minutes. Turn heat to low and add nut milk. Cook until desired consistency.

Number of Servings: 2

Prep Time: 15 minutes

Personal Notes: A great way to break fast for Vata and Pitta individuals. Kapha individuals can have it for dinner as well.

Mung Dahl Pancakes (Tridoshic)

1/2 c Mung Dahl powder
1 c water
1/2 tsp Himalayan salt
1/2 tsp fresh cilantro, chopped
1/4 tsp cumin seeds
1/2 tsp garam masala
1/4 tsp fenugreek powder
1/2 tsp ginger, grated
1/2 T Ghee or sesame oil

Mix powder and water to make pancake batter consistency (you may need a little more or less water). Use a preheated cast iron griddle. Add a few drops of Ghee or sesame oil. Pour the batter on the griddle into small pancakes. Cook thoroughly on one side and then flip. Cook thoroughly on the other side and remove. Serve warm with honey or chutney (See Sauces, Spice Mixes & Chutneys)

Number of Servings: 3

Prep Time: 20 minutes

Poha (Flattened rice)

1 small onion, diced
1-2 gloves garlic, diced
1/2 tsp ginger, grated
1/2 tsp mustard seeds
1/2 tsp turmeric
1/2 tsp black pepper
1/2 tsp garam masala
1/4 tsp fenugreek
A few curry leaves
1 c flattened rice (Thick Poha)
2 radishes, diced
1 small zucchini, diced
1/2 c broccoli, diced
1-2 carrots, diced
1 tsp lemon juice
1/4 c walnuts toasted
1/4 c fresh coriander

Soak Thick Poha (Flattened rice) in warm water for 5 minutes. Sauté mustard seeds until they start to pop, then add onion. Cook until translucent, then add garlic, ginger and all spices. Sauté 3-4 minutes and then add veggies. Sauté 10 minutes. Add rice and mix well. Add walnuts and fresh coriander just before serving.

Number of Servings: 4

Prep Time: 25 minutes

Personal Notes: A great way to break fast for Vata and Pitta individuals. Kapha individuals can have it for lunch.

Spiced Oatmeal with Seeds and Nuts

1/3 cup steel cut oatmeal
1 1/2 c water
Spice mixture:
1/2 T chia seeds
1/2 T hemp seeds
1/2 T flax seeds
1/2 T cinnamon
1/2 tsp cloves
1/2 tsp cardamom
Dash of black pepper, Hing and ginger powder
2 T almonds
1/4 c raisins

Put all ingredients except raisins in a pressure cooker and heat manually for 10 minutes. When finished, top with raisins and serve. Alternatively, cook on your stove top, bringing everything to a boil, then letting it simmer for 20 minutes. Top with raisins before serving. Try it with a 1/3 cup of Quinoa or a mix of quinoa & oats also.

Number of Servings: 2

Prep Time: 25 minutes

Personal Notes: A great way to break fast for Vata and Pitta individuals. Kapha individuals should use this recipe for brunch or dinner.

BOWLS

6 Tastes Wild Rice Bowl

3 stalks broccoli, stalks peeled
1 tsp extra virgin olive oil
1 T lemon juice
1 1/3 c wild rice
2 3/4 c water
2 purple beets, diced
2 tsp dried basil
1 tsp coconut amino acids
1 c greens of your choice
1 avocado
1/3 c walnuts, lightly toasted
1 tsp dried sage
2 T CCF spice mix (Recipe in Sauces, Spice Mixes &
  Chutneys)
2 T sun-dried tomatoes in olive oil
3 T olive oil
Sea salt and black pepper to taste
Mustard Ginger Dressing: (Recipe in Dips, Dressings &
  Drinks)

Preheat oven to 350°. Toast walnuts, sage and CCF spice mix in a skillet with 1 T olive oil for a couple minutes. Set aside. Line baking sheet with parchment paper. Put beets and broccoli on the pan and bake 30 minutes. Sprinkle with olive oil, lemon juice, basil, coconut amino, salt and pepper. Put rice in a saucepan and cover with water. Bring to a boil, add salt and simmer until liquid is absorbed. Take off the heat and set aside. To assemble: Place the greens, then rice, beets and broccoli in a bowl. Top with avocado slices, walnuts, sun dried tomatoes. Drizzle with Mustard Ginger dressing.

Number of Servings: 4

Prep Time: 20 minutes plus bake time

Personal Notes: Most Bowl recipes are Tridoshic. Generally speaking, bowls are best for lunchtime. Kapha individuals can use broth instead of olive oil.

Kale & Cranberry Bowl

1 bunch kale, ribs and stems removed, chopped
1/4 head of cabbage, shredded
1/4 c cranberries
1 avocado, sliced
1/4 cup nuts of your choice
1/4 c cooked grain of your choice (rice, quinoa, barley)
Vegan Poppy Seed Dressing (Recipe in Dips, Dressings
 & Drinks)

Toss kale with olive oil and massage it into the kale leaves for 30 seconds. Add the cabbage to the kale mixture. To assemble: Arrange the greens in a bowl with the avocado, nuts and grain of your choice. Top the salad with the cranberries and Vegan Poppy Seed dressing.

Number of Servings: 2

Prep Time: 10 minutes

Personal Notes: Most Bowl recipes are Tridoshic. Generally speaking, bowls are best for lunchtime. Kapha individuals can use broth instead of olive oil in the dressing.

Kale Quinoa Bowl

1 c cooked quinoa
1 sweet potato, diced
2 c kale, ribs and stems removed, chopped
4 oz tempeh
4 T soy sauce
1 T rice vinegar
1 T maple syrup
1/2 T olive oil
Dijon Lemon Tahini Dressing (Recipe in Dips, Dressings & Drinks)

Preheat oven 350°. Roast sweet potato cubes about 30 minutes on a parchment paper lined baking pan. Chop tempeh into 1 inch cubes. Steam in a double boiler or steam pot about 10 minutes. Marinade the tempeh in soy sauce, rice vinegar, maple syrup and olive oil for 30 minutes, then bake it at 425° for 10 minutes. Assemble bowl: Layer kale in the bowl and top with quinoa, cubed sweet potato, tempeh and dressing.

Number of Servings: 2

Prep Time: 15 minutes plus baking times

Personal Notes: Most Bowl recipes are Tridoshic. Generally speaking, bowls are best for lunchtime. Kapha individuals can use broth instead of olive oil. This bowl is better for Vata and Pitta individuals.

Rainbow Salad Bowl

Salad:
4 c baby spinach
1 1/2 c diced sweet potato
2 c cooked quinoa
1 can drained/rinsed chickpeas
1/2 c toasted almonds, slivered
1 c shredded red cabbage
1 large diced apple
1 diced avocado
Rainbow Dressing (Recipe in Dips, Dressings & Drinks)

Preheat oven to 350°. Place diced sweet potato on a parchment paper line baking sheet and bake for 30 minutes. Prepare the rest of the ingredients and then assemble. Place greens in a bowl and top with quinoa, sweet potato, cabbage, chickpeas, apples, avocado and almonds. Drizzle with dressing.

Number of Servings: 4

Prep Time: 25 minutes plus bake times

Personal Notes: Most Bowl recipes are Tridoshic. Generally speaking, bowls are best for lunchtime. Kapha individuals can use broth instead of olive oil.

Salmon with Rice Bowl

2 salmon filets, fresh, wild caught
1 T Ghee
Sea salt and black pepper
1 c spring greens
1 c black rice or wild rice
1/2 fresh lemon
Orange Ginger Dressing (Recipe in Dips, Dressings &
  Drinks)

Prepare rice and set aside. Make dressing and marinade salmon in 1/2 of it for 30 minutes. Heat a skillet with Ghee. Season salmon with salt and pepper. Place salmon in heated pan, skin side down. Cook 4 minutes on each side. Assemble bowl: Lay spring greens in a shallow bowl, layer with rice, salmon, sprinkle with lemon and remaining dressing.

Number of Servings: 2

Prep Time: 10 minutes plus cook times

Personal Notes: Wonderful recipe for Vata and Pitta individuals who are still eating animal proteins.

Spinach & Tempeh Bowl

1 c spinach, torn into bite size pieces
1/2 c arugula
1 c barley, cooked
1/2 c nuts of your choice
1/4 c seeds of your choice
1 package of flavored tempeh
Avocado Ranch Dressing (Recipe in Dips, Dressings &
  Drinks)

Cook tempeh and barley according to package. Make
Avocado Ranch dressing. Assemble bowl: Lay spinach
and arugula in a shallow bowl, layer with cooked barley,
tempeh, and top with your favorite nuts and seeds.
Drizzle dressing over the top.

Number of Servings: 2

Prep Time: 10 minutes plus cook times

Personal Notes: Most Bowl recipes are Tridoshic.
Generally speaking, bowls are best for lunchtime. Kapha
individuals can use broth instead of olive oil and this
bowl is specially good for them.

Tempeh Bowl

1 c farro
2 c veggie broth
1 pkg tempeh, cut into 1/2 inch strips
1 oz Soy sauce
1 tsp garam masala
1/2 tsp sea salt
2 avocados
1/2 c walnuts, chopped
4 oz arugula or kale
1 1/2 c veggie broth
1 T garlic powder
1/2 tsp garam masala
1/2 tsp sea salt
Dash of Hing
Avocado Ranch Dressing (Recipe in Dressings, Dips &
  Drinks)

Preheat oven to 350°. In a saucepan, cook farro in 2 cups of broth, covered, for 30 minutes. Set aside. Steam tempeh in a double boiler or steam pot for 10 minutes. Sprinkle tempeh with Soy sauce and garam masala. Bake on a baking sheet lined with parchment paper for 20-25 minutes. Boil veggie broth, then add spices and kale, cook for 2 minutes. To assemble: Place kale in 4 separate bowls, spooning a bit of the water it's cooked in over it. Drain farro and lay over kale. Lay tempeh slices, walnuts and avocado on top. Top with Avocado Ranch Dressing (see recipe in Dips, Dressings & Drinks)

Number of Servings: 4

Prep Time: 25 minutes plus baking times

Personal Notes: Most Bowls are Tridoshic and best at

lunch. Kaphas can use broth instead of olive oil.

Tofu Bowl

1 cup greens of your choice
1/4 c onion, diced
1/2 tsp ginger, diced
1 clove garlic, diced
1/2 tsp garam masala
1 avocado
1/4 c nuts of your choice
1 sweet potato, cooked
1/2 package tofu, any flavor
1 T extra virgin olive oil
Sea salt and black pepper to taste
Anti-Inflammatory Turmeric dressing (Recipe in Dips,
  Dressings & Drinks)

Preheat oven to 350°. Slice tofu and place on a baking sheet covered with parchment paper. Sprinkle with olive oil and bake 15-20 minutes. Heat Ghee in a skillet and add onions, ginger, garlic and garam masala, sauté for 3 minutes. Add greens, salt and pepper and combine well, cook 1 minute. Assemble bowl: Layer the greens with tofu, avocado, nuts and top with Anti-Inflammatory Turmeric Dressing. Serve the sweet potato on the side. Optional toppings: Hummus, pumpkin or sunflower seeds.

Number of Servings: 2

Prep Time: 20 minutes

Personal Notes: Most Bowl recipes are Tridoshic. Generally speaking, bowls are best for lunchtime. Kapha individuals can use broth instead of olive oil. This bowl is better for Vata and Pitta individuals.

SOUPS & STEWS

6 Tastes Chickpea Soup

1 can organic chickpeas, rinsed and drained
2 c veggie broth
3 c water
3 T leeks, sliced
1 tsp ground cumin
1 tsp coriander
1 tsp fennel seeds
1 tsp Dijon mustard
2 tsp tomato paste
2 carrots, thinly sliced
1/2 c greens, chopped
1 zucchini, sliced
1 T coconut aminos
1/2 tsp black pepper & sea salt
2 T lime juice
1 c coconut milk
2 T fresh cilantro
Optional: pinch of saffron, toppings: watercress or
  sunflower sprouts

Sauté cumin, coriander, fennel and leeks in a large skillet with 2 T of broth for 2-3 minutes. Add all ingredients except coconut milk, cilantro and toppings to the skillet. Bring to a boil, reduce heat and simmer 15 minutes. Add the coconut milk, salt and pepper to taste. Mix and simmer 5 minutes. Add broth to desired consistency. Add cilantro and optional toppings before serving.

Number of Servings: 4

Prep Time: 45 minutes

Personal Notes: Great for Vata and Pitta in cooler weather.

African Yam Stew

1 small onion, chopped
1/2 T ground ginger
1/2 T garlic, minced
1 tsp ground cumin
1 tsp ground coriander
Dash of crushed red pepper
3 yams, peeled and chopped
1 c water
12 oz tomatoes, diced
1/2 can garbanzo beans, drained & rinsed
1/2 can black eyed peas, drained & rinsed
1/4 c unsweetened nut butter
3/4 c corn
1/2 bunch kale, chopped
1/2 tsp black pepper

Over medium heat, sauté onion, garlic, ginger, cumin, coriander and red pepper for 2-3 minutes, stirring often. Add yams, water, tomatoes, beans, peas and nut butter. Bring to a boil, reduce heat and simmer for 20 minutes. Stir in corn, black pepper and greens and cook 10 minutes or until vegetables are tender.

Number of Servings: 3-4

Prep Time: 45 minutes

Personal Notes: Wonderful recipe for Vata and Pitta individuals in cooler, dryer weather.

Beets & Leeks Soup

3 large beets, skinned and diced
1 T coconut oil
1/2 tsp Himalayan salt
1 large leek, cleaned and sliced into 1/2 inch pieces
1/2 clove garlic, minced
1 13 oz can of coconut milk
1/2 tsp turmeric
1/2 tsp garam masala
1/4 tsp black pepper
2 c vegetable broth

Sauté beets and leeks in coconut oil for 10-12 minutes. Add turmeric, masala and pepper, garlic, and salt. Simmer for 8 minutes. Add coconut milk and vegetable broth, mix well. Put in a blender and pulse until desired consistency or use an immersion blender.

Number of Servings: 4

Prep Time: 25 min

Personal Notes: This soup is good for Pitta and Kapha individuals. Vata individuals may add cooked quinoa to the recipe if desired.

Bok Choy Soup (Tridoshic)

1 1/2 bunches baby bok choy, cleaned and chopped
1/4 c lime juice
1 tsp coconut oil
1 tsp fresh ginger, grated
2 garlic cloves, minced
1/2 tsp lemon zest
1/2 tsp lime zest
1 tsp fresh turmeric, grated
1/4 c water
1 can coconut milk
1/4 tsp sea salt
2 oz mung bean vermicelli (optional)
1 red Thai pepper, diced or 1T red pepper flakes
 (optional)
Cilantro OR diced scallions and sesame seeds
1 package tofu, pan seared with 1 green onion and 1
 clove minced garlic

Heat the coconut oil over medium high heat. Add the ginger, garlic, lemon and lime zest, turmeric and red pepper if desired. Cook 2 minutes, then add the lime juice and chopped bok choy. Cook another 2 minutes. Add the water, coconut milk, salt and simmer for 5 minutes. Separately, pan sear sliced tofu in olive oil, garlic and green onion about 5 minutes or until lightly browned. Mix tofu into the soup, add salt and pepper to taste. If desired, cook vermicelli according to package and drain. To serve, put soup over the vermicelli, garnish with scallions, sesame seeds, cilantro if desired.

Number of Servings: 4

Prep Time: 30 minutes

Chilean Bean Stew

1 large yellow onion, diced
4 clove garlic, minced
1 medium butternut squash, peeled, seeded, 1/2 inch
 cubes
1 can pinto beans drained and rinsed
1 tsp garam masala
3 1/2 c fresh or frozen corn kernels
Sea salt and black pepper to taste
1 c fresh basil, chopped
1/4 cup vegetable broth
2 c water

In a saucepan on medium to high heat, sauté the onion, stirring until translucent, about 3 minutes. Add broth to deglaze the pan. Lower the heat and add garlic, squash, beans, corn and water. Cook 25 minutes or until squash is tender. Remove from heat, add salt, pepper and stir in the basil.

Number of Servings: 4

Prep Time: 30 minutes

Personal Notes: Wonderful recipe for Vata and Pitta individuals in cooler weather.

Ginger, Carrot, Squash Soup

1 small butternut squash chunks, peeled, seeded
2 medium carrots, chopped
1 medium red onion, chopped
1 tsp cumin
1 tsp coriander powder
1 tsp turmeric
1 tsp Himalayan salt
2 tsp ginger, grated
1/2 tsp garam masala
4 1/4 c veggie broth
1/2 T Ghee or coconut oil
1 14 oz can coconut milk
Cilantro, chopped as a garnish

Bake butternut squash at 350° for 30-40 minutes or until soft. Heat oil and sauté onion for 3-4 minutes. Add cumin, coriander and turmeric, sauté another 3-4 minutes. Add a little broth to the mixture if needed and sauté another few minutes. Add the squash, carrots and broth and cook for 10 minutes. Add salt, ginger, garam masala and take off the heat. Use an immersion blender to mix until desired consistency or use a blender on low speed. Add the can of coconut milk and heat until warm. Top with chopped cilantro,

Number of Servings: 3

Prep Time: 15 minutes plus baking times

Personal Notes: Excellent recipe for Pitta and Kapha individuals. Kapha individuals can make it with broth in place of coconut oil.

Irish Stew

3 stalks celery, chopped
1 small onion, diced
6 c vegetable broth
4 Yukon gold potatoes, quartered
4 carrots, chopped
12 oz tempeh, cut into 1 inch pieces
2 T tomato paste, no salt added
2 tsp dried thyme
2 c cabbage, chopped
1/4 c red wine vinegar
Sea salt and black pepper to taste
1/2 bunch fresh parsley, finely chopped
1/2 bunch chives, finely chopped

Dry sauté the onion and celery until onion is translucent. Add the broth, potatoes, tempeh, carrots, tomato paste and dried thyme. Bring to a boil and reduce heat, simmer 20 minutes. Add the cabbage, vinegar, and herbs. Cook until cabbage and potatoes are tender.

Number of Servings: 4

Prep Time: 30 minutes

Personal Notes: Wonderful recipe for Vata and Pitta individuals in cooler weather.

Kitchari (Tridoshic)

6 c water
1 c whole green mung, soaked and drained
3/4 c rice or quinoa
1 small onion, diced
1 clove garlic, diced
1 stalk celery, diced
1-2 carrots, diced
1 T ginger, grated
2 T fresh lemon or lime juice
1 T Ghee
1 T mustard seeds
1 tsp turmeric
1/2 tsp black pepper
1 tsp ground coriander
1 tsp Himalayan salt
3 1/2 c bok choy, kale or spinach
4 tsp cilantro

In an Instant Pot, heat Ghee and add mustard seeds. When the seeds begin to pop, add garlic, celery, onion and rest of spices, sauté for 10 minutes. Add the carrot, rice and whole green mung, mix well. Add lemon/lime juice. Set Instant Pot on Manual for 30 minutes. When finished, add the greens and let sit for 5 minutes. Top with cilantro.

Number of Servings: 4-5

Prep Time: 40 minutes

Personal Notes: You can use split or yellow mung in place of whole mung. Use whatever veggies you have with the onion and celery, (carrots, radishes, asparagus, etc). Kitchari is very versatile and has excellent nutrition.

Lentil Soup (Tridoshic)

2/3 c lentils, rinsed well (horsegram, red lentil or green
  mung)
1/3 c carrots, diced
1/3 c celery, diced
1/3 c green beans
4 bay leaves
1/3 c kale or spinach
1/8 c cilantro, chopped
3 1/3 c water
1 tsp coconut oil
1 T mustard seeds
1 tsp turmeric
1/2 tsp black pepper
1/4 tsp Hing
1 tsp coriander
1 tsp Himalayan salt

Heat coconut oil in the pressure cooker, add mustard seeds and sauté until they begin to pop. Add other spices and heat 5 minutes. Add lentils, carrots, celery and green beans and cook according to what you've used: Horsegram-45 minutes, red lentils-20 minutes, green mung-30 minutes. Remove bay leaves. Add the cilantro and spinach or kale just before serving.

Number of Servings: 4

Prep Time: 15 minutes plus cook time

Personal Notes: Vata individuals can add root vegetables like potatoes or sweet potatoes.

Miso Soup

2 tsp coconut oil
3 slices fresh ginger, minced
1 large onion, sliced thin
2 carrots, peeled and sliced thin
2 stalks celery, sliced thin
4 c cabbage, chopped
5 c water
4-5 inches dried seaweed
1/4 c diced tofu
4 T miso (light or dark)
2 green onions, chopped
1 tsp roasted sesame oil

Heat coconut oil, add ginger and onion. Sauté 5 minutes, then add carrots, celery, tofu, seaweed and cabbage. Stir well. Add water, bring to a boil, then reduce heat and simmer about 10 minutes, until carrots are tender. Remove from heat. Place miso in a bowl, add a little broth from the soup and make a smooth paste. Add it to the soup. Let it rest for 5 minutes. Place chopped green onions and a few drops of sesame oil on top before serving.

Number of Servings: 4

Prep Time: 15 minutes plus cook time.

Personal Notes: Great recipe for Vata and Kapha individuals.

Quinoa Bean and Kale Stew

Herb Blend:
1/4 tsp fennel seeds, crushed
1/2 tsp dried marjoram
1/2 tsp dried thyme
1/4 tsp rosemary
Fresh ground black pepper

1 c onions, thinly sliced
1/2 tsp sea salt
2 garlic cloves, minced
1 large carrot, diced
2 c veggie broth
2 c water
3/4 lb Yukon gold potatoes, diced
1/2 c quinoa, rinsed
1/2 can white beans, drained and rinsed
1/2 bunch kale, stems removed, torn into bite size pieces

Mix herb blend ingredients in a bowl, stir and set aside. Preheat large pot over medium high heat. Sauté onions and garlic in 2 tablespoons of salted water for 3 minutes. Add the carrot and herb blend and sauté 1 minute. Add the broth, water, potatoes and quinoa. Cover and bring to a boil. Reduce heat and simmer 15 minutes or until the potatoes and quinoa are tender. Add the kale and beans and simmer 5 minutes until kale is wilted. Add a dash of lemon juice, balsamic vinegar or hot sauce before serving.

Number of Servings: 4

Prep Time: 30 minutes

Personal Notes: Good for Vata and Pitta in cool weather.

Spinach & Kale Soup

1/2 c spinach
1/2 c kale, stems and ribs removed
1 c carrots, chopped
3 stalks asparagus, chopped OR 1/2 cup green beans
1 small stalk celery, diced
1/2 c quinoa
4 c vegetable broth
2 inches ginger, grated
1/2 tsp turmeric
1/2 tsp garam masala
1/2 tsp black pepper
1/2 tsp sea salt
1/2 lemon
Dash of Hing
1 T coconut oil

Sauté spices in coconut oil. Add broth, quinoa and vegetables (except spinach and kale). Simmer for 1/2 hour. Add spinach and kale and heat through before serving.

Number of Servings: 4

Prep Time: 45 minutes

Personal Notes: Excellent soup for Pitta and Kapha individuals.

Sweet Potato Soup

3 medium sweet potatoes
1 large onion
4 c veggie broth
1 T Ghee
Dash of Himalayan salt
3 tsp coriander
2 inches ginger, chopped
1 tsp turmeric
1/2 tsp black pepper
1/2 tsp garam masala
1 bunch fresh coriander

Boil sweet potatoes until tender, peel and cut into bite size cubes. Sauté onion in Ghee for a minute, add spices and cook 2 minutes. Add the broth and sweet potatoes to the spice mix and simmer 10 minutes, then add salt. Put into a blender and process until smooth. Garnish with fresh coriander leaves.

Number of Servings: 4

Prep Time: 45 minutes

Personal Notes: Wonderful recipe for Vata and Pitta individuals in cooler weather.

Vegan Creamy Cauliflower Mushroom Soup

2 c fresh or frozen cauliflower florets, cooked until
 tender and drained
1 T olive oil
1 pound of mushrooms, washed, dried and sliced
1 large onion, diced
1/2 tsp dried thyme
1/2 tsp dried basil
1/2 tsp dried oregano
1/4 tsp rosemary
1/4 tsp sage
1/4 tsp marjoram
3 cloves garlic, minced
2 cup vegetable broth
1 1/2 water
2/3 c raw cashews (soaked, drained)
2 T nutritional yeast
1 T fresh lemon juice
1 tsp sea salt & black pepper to taste

Heat olive oil, add mushrooms, onion, and all spices.
Sauté 5 minutes, stirring often. Add garlic and cook 1
minute. Add broth and bring to a boil. Reduce heat,
simmer, covered for10 minutes. Purée cauliflower in a
blender with water, cashews, yeast, salt, lemon juice on
high for 2 minutes until smooth and creamy. Add
cauliflower to the soup and mix. Simmer 6-7 minutes or
until it starts to thicken. Salt and pepper to taste.

Number of Servings: 4

Prep Time: 30 minutes

Personal Notes: Great for Pitta and Kapha individuals.
Vata can add root vegetables like sweet potato.

Vegan Kale Soup

3 c vegetable broth
1/2 T garlic, finely diced
1/2 c onion, diced
1 small turnip, diced
1 carrot, diced
1 bunch kale, roughly chopped, stems and ribs removed
1-2 bay leaves
1 1/2 T fresh parsley, chopped
1 T fresh thyme, chopped
1 can kidney beans, rinsed and drained
1 medium potato, diced
1 c split peas, cooked in water and drained

When split peas are done, purée them in a blender and set aside. In a large stock pot, heat a couple tablespoons of broth. Add the garlic, onions, turnips and carrots. Cook 5 minutes. Add the rest of the stock, bay leaf, parsley, thyme and potatoes. Mix well and simmer 10 minutes. Add the beans, kale and puréed split peas. Add water to desired consistency. Bring to a boil, reduce heat and simmer 30-40 minutes. Remove bay leaf.

Number of Servings: 3-4

Prep Time: 45 minutes

Personal Notes: Excellent for Pitta and Kapha individuals.

Vegetable Quinoa Stew

1 small onion, diced
2 small carrots, diced
1 1/2 stalks celery, diced
1 large sweet potato, diced
1 small butternut squash, diced
1/2 can chickpeas, rinsed and drained
6 T quinoa
14 oz can diced tomatoes
1-2 bay leaves
1-2 cloves of garlic, diced
1/2 T fresh rosemary
1 tsp fresh thyme
1 tsp garam masala
2 c vegetable broth
1 c kale, chopped, stems and ribs removed
Sea salt and black pepper to taste

Place all ingredients, except kale, in an Instant Pot. Cook on soup setting for 30 minutes. Add kale and manually cook another 10 minutes. Let sit 10 minutes before serving.

Number of Servings: 5-6

Prep Time: 55 minutes

Personal Notes: Wonderful recipe for Vata and Pitta individuals in cooler weather.

Vegetable Soup

1 medium onion, chopped
2 stalks celery, chopped
1 c tomatoes, chopped
1 c cabbage, chopped
1/4 c red lentils, rinsed
1/2 c brown rice, rinsed
1/4 package frozen mixed veggies
1 c potatoes, chopped
1/4 c okra, chopped
2 tsp CCF spice mix (Recipe in Sauces, Spice Mixes & Chutneys)
1 small bottle organic tomato juice
3 c water

Sauté onion and celery in a little water for about 3 minutes. Add lentils and rice and cook 5 minutes. Add all other ingredients and simmer about 45 minutes or until veggies are all cooked.

Number of Servings: 4

Prep Time: 55 minutes

Personal Notes: Tridoshic but best for Pitta and Kapha individuals.

Veggie Broth

4 c hot water
1 onion, quartered
1 carrot, chopped
1 stalk celery, chopped
1 bay leaf
1 tsp salt and black pepper
All veggie peelings from past week

Place all ingredients in Instant Pot or pressure cooker. Set to broth/soup setting for 30 minutes. Strain out veggies and keep broth in the fridge. This broth can be used in place of water in almost everything to add taste and nutrition. During the week, collect peelings from veggies, ends, stalks from greens, etc. and use them for this recipe.

Number of Servings: 2 cups

Prep Time: 35 minutes

Warming Winter Soup

1 T Ghee
1/2 onion, diced
1 small carrot, sliced
1 parsnip, sliced
1 c butternut squash, chopped
1 c cabbage, chopped
3 c vegetable broth
2 tsp CCF spice mix
1 tsp garam masala
1 tsp sea salt and black pepper
1 tsp fresh rosemary
1 tsp fresh thyme
1/4 c riced cauliflower
1 T dry white wine (optional)

Heat Ghee and sauté the onions until translucent. Add salt, spices and carrot. Add each vegetable one by one in the order they appear, allowing each one to heat and sweat before adding the next. After all the vegetables are added, continue to sauté until they begin to stick to the bottom of the pan. Add the fresh herbs, deglaze with the wine or a little water. Scrape up any sticky parts, add salt and pepper to taste. Add the broth and riced cauliflower. Bring to a boil, reduce heat and simmer, covered, for at least 30 minutes.

Number of Servings: 3-4

Prep Time: 55 minutes

Personal Notes: Wonderful recipe for Vata and Pitta individuals in cooler weather.

MAIN ENTREES

Ayurvedic Macaroni and No Cheese

1/2 c frozen butternut squash, thawed, mashed
3/4 c nut milk
1 T arrowroot or cornstarch
4 T nutritional yeast
1 T Dijon mustard
1/2 tsp garlic powder
1/4 tsp lemon juice
1/4 tsp sea salt
Dash of black pepper
6 oz macaroni noodles
1/2 c peas
1 c spinach

Preheat oven to 350°. Place the butternut squash, milk, arrowroot, nutritional yeast, mustard, garlic powder, lemon juice, salt and pepper in a blender. Blend until smooth and creamy. Transfer to a saucepan and whisk over medium heat until thickened. Cook pasta according to directions. Combine the pasta, sauce, spinach and peas in a casserole dish. Bake uncovered for 20-30 minutes until golden brown and bubbly.

Number of Servings: 4

Prep Time: 20 minutes plus cook time

Personal Notes: Great for Vata individuals.

Ayurvedic Pizza

6 organic whole wheat flour tortillas
2 c pizza sauce or pesto (if using pesto, then delete the
 spices below)
3/4 c broccoli florets
1/2 lb organic tofu, crumbled
1 1/2 c fresh organic mozzarella cheese
1/2 c olives, chopped
1/4 tsp turmeric
1/4 tsp ground ginger
1/8 black pepper
1/8 ground coriander
1 T extra virgin olive oil
Oregano to garnish

Preheat oven to 350º. Steam broccoli and tofu until tender and salt to taste. Pulse in a blender until smooth, set aside. In a skillet, heat the tortillas 30-40 seconds on each side over medium heat. If using pizza sauce, stir in the spices, except the oregano and set aside. Place 3 tortillas on a baking pan. Spread a thin layer of cheese over each tortilla and then place another tortilla on top. This makes a thicker crust and makes it easier to eat. Brush the top tortilla with olive oil. Spread with a layer of pizza sauce or pesto, then a thin layer of the tofu/broccoli mixture over the sauce. Top with cheese. Garnish with olives and a pinch of oregano. Bake 10 minutes or until cheese is melted.

Number of Servings: 3

Prep Time: 15 minutes plus cook time

Personal Notes: Great for Vata individuals. Pitta and Kapha individuals can have one serving as a side dish.

Chickpea Cauliflower & Rice (Tridoshic)

1 can chickpeas, rinsed and drained
2 T water
1/2 c raw cashews, chopped, lightly toasted
3/4 T coconut oil
1 c yellow onion, diced
1/2 T ginger, grated
1 tsp mustard seeds
3/4 tsp sea salt
1 tsp cumin, ground
1/2 tsp turmeric, ground
1/4 tsp cardamom, ground
1/2 tsp black pepper
1 clove garlic, grated
3 c cauliflower, trimmed and cut into 1 inch pieces
1 c carrots, chopped
1/2 can coconut milk
3/4 T Tamari
1 c basmati or jasmine rice, cooked
Optional toppings: cilantro, 1/2 lime, sriracha sauce

In a large pot, heat coconut oil; add onion, ginger, pepper, mustard seeds and sea salt. Cook 5 minutes, stirring often. Add cumin, turmeric, cardamom, garlic and a bit of water. Cook on low 5 minutes, stirring often. Add carrots, cauliflower and water. Cover and cook on low 15 minutes, until veggies are tender. Add chickpeas and coconut milk. Stir to mix, cook 5 minutes. Stir in the cashews and Tamari. Serve over rice with optional toppings if desired.

Number of Servings: 3-4

Prep Time: 30 minutes

Easy Veggie Empanadas

Filling:
1 c spinach
1/2 c diced potato
1 onion, finely chopped
1 c protein, e.g. soy crumbles or tofu
Dash of soy sauce
1/4 c veggie broth
1 tsp garam masala
1 tsp sea salt
Dough:
3 c whole wheat flour
1/2 c cornstarch or arrowroot
2 tsp sea salt
1 c cold water
1/4 c extra virgin olive oil

Preheat oven to 400°. Mix the filling ingredients, except spinach, in a large pot. Simmer on medium heat, covered, for 20 minutes. Add spinach. Set aside to cool. To make dough: In a bowl, mix flour, cornstarch and salt. Add water and oil and kneed for 5 minutes. Place on a lightly floured surface, roll into a thin sheet and cut into 6 inch circles. Put a spoonful of filling in each circle but don't overfill. Wet the edges of the dough with water and fold over to form a pocket. Crimp the edges with a fork. Line a baking sheet with parchment paper and place the empanadas in a row, not touching. Bake 25 minutes, until golden brown. Serve with any chutney (Recipes in Sauces, Spice Mixes & Chutneys).

Number of Servings: 4

Prep Time: 30 minutes plus cook time

Personal Notes: Great for Vata individuals. Pitta and Kapha individuals can have it as a side dish.

Eggplant

3 Japanese eggplants or one large regular eggplant, cut
  into chunks
2 1/2 T oil of your choice
3/4 tsp salt
1 clove garlic, minced
1 T onion, minced
1 T ginger, grated
1/2 c fresh mushrooms
1/2 c bean sprouts
1 T hoisin sauce
1 T soy sauce
1/2 tsp black pepper
1/2 tsp toasted sesame oil
2 green onions, sliced thinly
Handful of cilantro, coarsely chopped
1 tsp sesame seeds, slightly dry toasted

Sprinkle eggplant with salt and let sit for 10 minutes, then rinse. Heat oil and add garlic. When the garlic is brown take it out & put it aside, leaving as much oil as possible in the pan. Add the onion and eggplant, cook 5 minutes. Add the green onions, ginger, and mushrooms. Stir in hoisin and soy sauce and cook until the sauce thickens. Check the eggplant and cook until it is tender. Add the bean sprouts, garlic, onions, cilantro and black pepper and toss well. Take off the heat and let stand for 5 minutes. Garnish with toasted sesame seeds.

Number of Servings: 3

Prep Time: 40 minutes

Personal Notes: Great for Vata Individuals. Pitta and Kapha individuals can have as a side dish.

Lentil Loaf with Vegan Gravy (Tridoshic)

1 c dried lentils
2 c veggie broth
1 small onion, finely chopped
1 carrot, finely chopped
2 stalks celery, finely chopped
1/4 c tomato sauce
2 T yellow mustard
2 T low sodium soy sauce
2 T nutritional yeast
1 T Italian seasoning
1/2 teaspoon Himalayan salt
1 c rice, cooked
Vegan Gravy (Recipe in Sauces, Spice Mixes & Chutneys)

Preheat oven to 350º. Combine lentils with veggie broth and bring to a boil. Reduce heat and simmer 20 minutes or until lentils are soft but not mushy. Put onion, carrot, and celery in a bowl and mix with tomato sauce, mustard, soy, yeast and seasonings. Set aside. Put the lentils in a blender and pulse a few times. Combine the lentils and cooked rice in a bowl. Pour the two mixes together and mix well. Line a bread pan with parchment paper and press the mixture into each corner, forming a loaf. Bake 40-50 minutes or until firm with a crispy outer layer. Let cool for 10 minutes before serving. Top with Vegan Gravy.

Number of Servings: 1 loaf

Prep Time: 25 minutes plus bake time

Penne Pasta with Peas & Mushrooms

1 small onion, chopped
1/2 lb wild or cremini mushrooms, thinly sliced
14 oz can diced tomatoes
1 c frozen green peas
1/2 c jarred marinara sauce
Sea salt, ground black pepper to taste
Crushed red pepper flakes to taste (optional)
8 oz penne pasta
1 T parsley

Bring a large pot of salted water to a boil. Cook pasta for 12 minutes, then drain. In a skillet, cook the onion until softened, 3-4 minutes. Add the mushrooms and stir for 1 minute. Add the tomatoes, marinara sauce, peas, salt and pepper and red pepper (optional). Bring to a boil, then reduce heat and simmer gently for 10 minutes. Add the pasta, mix well and top with parsley.

Number of Servings: 4

Prep Time: 15 minutes

Personal Notes: Great for Vata individuals. Pitta and Kapha individuals can have as a side dish.

Rice & Veggies Pulao (Tridoshic)

2 c basmati rice, soaked for 1/2 hour
1 carrot, cubed
2 large onions, sliced
1/2 c cauliflower florets
2 potatoes, cubed
1/4 c green peas
1 tsp grated ginger & 1 clove garlic made into a paste
1/2 tsp black pepper
2 1/2 c veggie broth
3 T Ghee
1/2 tsp sea salt
1 tsp cumin
1 bay leaf
2 cardamom pods
2 whole cloves
Pinch of mace
1 small star anise
1 inch cinnamon
1 lemon, cut into 8 wedges

Heat Ghee in a skillet and sauté 1/2 the onions. Take onion out and set it aside. In the same pan, sauté cumin, bay leaf, cloves, cardamoms, mace, anise, cinnamon until fragrant. Add the uncooked onion slices and sauté until brown. Add the ginger/garlic paste and cook 1 minute. Add the pepper and cauliflower, potatoes and peas. Sauté 2-3 minutes. Drain the rice and add it to the pan. Mix so everything is well coated, add broth and salt. Cover and cook until the rice is done. Let stand 5 minutes, garnish with cooked onions and lemon.

Number of Servings: 4

Prep Time: 20 minutes

Roasted Root Vegetables

1 large sweet potato, cubed
4 purple or red potatoes, cubed
2 beets, cubed
2 large carrots, sliced, bite size
1 T chaat masala
4 cloves garlic, chopped
1 large onion, sliced
2 T coconut oil
1 tsp ginger, minced
1 tsp lemon juice
Salt & pepper to taste
Toppings: fresh coriander and a sprinkle of oregano

Preheat oven to 400°. Put all the veggies in a bowl and toss with chaat masala, coconut oil, garlic, onion, ginger. Put parchment paper on a baking pan and place veggie in a single layer. Bake for 40 minutes. Turn veggies over halfway through. Add salt, pepper and lemon juice before serving. Top with coriander and oregano.

Number of Servings: 4

Prep Time: 15 minutes plus cook time

Personal Notes: Tridoshic but better for Vata and Pitta individuals.

Roasted Veggie Ratatouille

1 eggplant, large dice
1 zucchini, large dice
1 yellow squash, large dice
1 pint cherry tomatoes
3 garlic cloves, minced
5 basil leaves, torn
2 T extra virgin olive oil
Sea salt and black pepper to taste

Preheat oven to 425°. Put the cherry tomatoes on a baking sheet with 1 T of the olive oil, salt and pepper. Mix to coat and set aside. On a separate baking pan, add all the remaining ingredients, except the basil, and 1 T of olive oil, salt and pepper. Place both pans in the oven for 15 minutes or until desired tenderness. Remove pans and combine into one bowl. Add the basil leaves. Can be served as a side dish or over brown rice as an entree.

Number of Servings: 4

Prep Time: 15 minutes plus cook time

Personal Notes: Tridoshic but better for Pitta individuals. Kapha can use vegetable broth in place of olive oil.

Romesco Penne Pasta (Tridoshic)

1 c roasted red peppers
1 c roasted tomatoes
4 roasted garlic cloves
1/4 c tahini
1/4 c extra virgin olive oil
1 T red wine vinegar
1/4 c toasted hazelnuts, chopped
1/2 tsp sea salt
2 c chickpea pasta
Basil leaves for garnish

Preheat oven to 400°. Roast the red peppers, tomatoes and garlic until blistered and browned. Place this mixture in a blender and add tahini. Blend until desired thickness as your pasta sauce. Add salt, pepper, vinegar and drizzle in the olive oil. Gently stir in hazelnuts. Serve over pasta and top with basil leaves.

Number of Servings: 4

Prep Time: 15 minutes plus roasting time

Smashed Chickpea Salad Sandwich (Tridoshic)

1 can chickpeas, drained & rinsed
1/4 c + 1 T dill pickles, finely chopped
1/4 c onions, finely chopped
2 T Vegan mayonnaise
2 1/2 tsp stone ground mustard
1 1/2 tsp apple cider vinegar
Sea salt and black pepper to taste
2 tsp dill, chopped
1/8 tsp turmeric
Multigrain bread
Toppings: sprouts, kale, shredded carrots, lettuce,
  tomatoes

Roughly mash the chickpeas. Add the pickles, onion, mayo, mustard, vinegar, dill, turmeric, salt and pepper. Mix well. Pile onto bread and add your favorite toppings.

Number of Servings: 2-3

Prep Time: 10 minutes

Spicy Asian Tacos

1 large butternut squash, peeled, seeded, cut into cubes
1/2 c water
3 c oyster mushrooms, sliced
2 c broccoli florets
1 c thinly sliced carrots
2 T cornstarch
5 T low sodium tamari
6 garlic cloves, minced
1 T fresh ginger, grated
1 tsp turmeric powder
2 tsp rice vinegar
1 tsp crushed red pepper (optional)
4 c Swiss chard or other greens, chopped
1/2 tsp garam masala
1 tsp coriander powder
24 6 inch corn tortillas, warmed
1/4 c scallions, thinly sliced

Bring the squash and 1/4 cup water to a boil in a skillet. Reduce heat, cover, simmer 7 minutes. Stir in the mushrooms, broccoli, and carrots. Simmer, covered, 5 minutes. Combine the cornstarch, tamari, garlic, ginger, vinegar and crushed red pepper in a small bowl with 1/4 c water. Add the tamari mixture and the greens to the veggies, cook for 1 minute, adding a bit of water until desired consistency. Spoon into doubled tortillas and sprinkle with scallions.

Number of Servings: 4

Prep Time: 25 minutes

Personal Notes: Tridoshic but better for Pitta and Kapha individuals.

Thai Curry with Tofu

1 c firm tofu, cubed
1 large red onion, diced
1 lemon
1 T lemongrass paste
1 T coconut oil
1/2 c vegetable broth
2 large carrots, sliced
1 stalk celery, sliced
1 tsp cumin seeds
2 tsp coriander powder
2 tsp turmeric
1 tsp garam masala
1 tsp black salt
1 tsp mustard seeds
3 cloves garlic, diced
2 inches ginger, grated
1/4 tsp Hing
1 bunch fresh basil, chopped
4 c chopped vegetables of your choice (bok choy,
  mushrooms, corn, asparagus, zucchini, potatoes)
1 1/2 c black or white rice, cooked
1 can unsweetened coconut milk

Preheat oven to 400°. Bake tofu for 30 minutes, set aside. Mix juice from lemon and lemongrass into a paste, set aside. Sauté onion in oil for 2 minutes. Add veggie broth, carrots and celery, cumin, coriander, turmeric, garam masala, black salt and mustard seeds. Simmer 10 minutes, then add garlic, ginger, Hing, rest of vegetables and 1/2 can of coconut milk. Add the tofu and simmer 15 minutes. Add lemongrass mixture and other 1/2 can of coconut milk, cook 5 minutes. Serve over rice, topped with fresh basil.

Number of Servings: 4

Prep Time: 45 minutes

Personal Notes: Tridoshic but best for Vata individuals.

Vegan Chili Spinach Pie

2 T extra virgin olive oil
1 large red onion, finely chopped
2 garlic cloves, crushed
1 large carrot, chopped
1 15 oz can diced tomatoes
1 1/2 c veggie broth
1/2 c soy crumbles, prepared according to package
1/2 tsp black pepper
1/2 tsp chili powder
1 tsp cumin
1 can of beans of your choice
1 c fresh spinach, chopped
1 pre-made puff pastry sheet

Preheat oven to 400°. Over medium heat, in a large skillet, fry the onion and garlic until softened. Add the carrots and cook 2-3 more minutes. Add the diced tomatoes and veggie broth. Cover and simmer 10 minutes. Add the soy crumbles, pepper, chili powder, cumin and cook 5 minutes. Add the beans and spinach and mix well. Pour into a baking dish and cover with puff pastry sheet. Brush a little soy milk on top. Bake 40 minutes or until golden brown.

Number of Servings: 4

Prep Time: 15 minutes plus cook time

Personal Notes: Excellent for Vata individuals in cool weather. Pitta and Kapha individuals can have as a side dish.

Vegan Tacos with Corn Slaw

2 14 oz cans heart of palm, drained & rinsed
1 T Ghee
1 T lime juice
1/4 tsp chili powder
1/2 tsp ground cumin
1/4 tsp cayenne pepper (optional)
1/2 tsp granulated garlic
1/2 tsp sea salt
Cilantro-Lime Corn Slaw:
1/4 c vegan mayo
1-2 T lime juice
2 tsp agave or maple syrup
1/2 tsp black pepper
1/2 tsp granulated garlic
1/2 tsp sea salt
2 c purple cabbage, shredded
1 c frozen corn kernels, thawed
1/4 c cilantro, chopped
10 corn tortillas
1 avocado, peeled and cubed

Preheat oven to 425°. Line a baking pan with parchment paper. Add the hearts of palm to a food processor and pulse 2-3 times, until shredded, don't over-process. In a bowl, add Ghee, lime juice, chili powder, cumin, cayenne (if using), garlic and sea salt. Whisk and then add shredded hearts of palm to the mix and gently combine. Put this on a baking pan in one layer. Bake for 10-12 minutes or until lightly browned. Corn Slaw: Whisk together the mayo, lime juice, agave, garlic and salt. Add the cabbage, corn and cilantro. Combine well. To assemble: Heat tortilla in a skillet over medium heat for 30 seconds on each side. Top tortilla with the hearts of palm mix. Top with slaw and cubed avocado. Can be served with salsa, hot sauce, lime wedges or sour cream.

Number of Servings: 4-5

Prep Time: 20 minutes plus cook time

Personal Notes: Great dish for Vata and Pitta individuals. Kapha individuals can use vegetable broth in place of olive oil.

Vegan Vegetable Lasagna (Tridoshic)

2 T water
1/2 small onion, diced
1 c carrots, diced
1 c zucchini, diced
1 c yellow squash, diced
4 oz mushrooms, chopped
Dash of Italian seasonings
1/2 package frozen spinach, thawed and drained
1 1/2 c pasta sauce
4-5 no boil lasagna noodles
1 c vegan ricotta, cashew ricotta cheese or tofu ricotta
Sea salt and black pepper to taste
Almond Parmesan
Fresh basil leaves for garnish

Preheat oven to 375°. Sauté onions and garlic over medium heat in the water for about 5 minutes. Add carrots, zucchini, squash, mushrooms, seasonings, salt and pepper. Continue to sauté for another 5 minutes. Remove from heat. Mix the ricotta and spinach together. Use a 9 x 9 baking dish. Layer a little of the pasta sauce on the bottom, top with 1/2 lasagna noodles, top with 1/2 the ricotta/spinach mix and 1/2 the veggies. Add another layer of noodles, sauce, ricotta and veggies. Cover with the remaining sauce. Cover with foil, bake 35-40 minutes. Let rest, covered, for 5 minutes. Remove cover and let rest another 10 minutes. Sprinkle with Parmesan cheese and freshly chopped basil.

Number of Servings: 4-5

Prep Time: 20 minutes plus baking time

SIDE DISHES

Asian Wild Rice Salad (Tridoshic)

3 c wild rice, cooked and cooled
3 T green onion, sliced on the bias
1 c carrot, shredded
1 1/2 c cabbage, shredded
4 T fresh cilantro, chopped
3 T toasted sesame seeds
1 lime cut into wedges
Dressing: Asian Dressing (Recipe in Dips, Dressings &
  Drinks)

Place wild rice in a bowl with the onions, carrots, cabbage, cilantro and half the sesame seeds. Add the dressing and toss to mix. When serving, add the rest of the cilantro and squeeze a lime wedge over it.

Number of Servings: 4

Prep Time: 20 minutes

Personal Notes: Tridoshic but could be a main dish for Kapha individuals.

Barley Sauté (Tridoshic)

1 c barley
2 c water
1 tsp fresh ginger, minced
1 tsp fresh parsley, minced
2 tsp fresh basil, minced
2 T red bell pepper, diced
1/2 tsp turmeric
1/2 tsp mustard seeds
1/2 tsp fenugreek seeds
1/2 tsp cumin seeds
1 T olive oil

Bring water to a boil, add barley and reduce to low heat. Cover and cook 40 minutes or until water is absorbed. In a separate skillet, heat olive oil. Add the mustard seeds and when they pop, add the cumin and fenugreek. Cook for 1 minute. Add the ginger, turmeric and red pepper. Cook 3 minutes and then add the barley. Combine and cook for a few more minutes. Garnish with parsley and basil and salt to taste.

Number of Servings: 2

Prep Time: 10 minutes plus cook time

Personal Notes: Tridoshic but could be a main dish for Kapha individuals.

Chickpeas with Spinach & Sun Dried Tomatoes (Tridoshic)

1 yellow onion, diced
4 garlic cloves, minced
1 T fresh ginger, minced
1 lemon (juice and zest)
1/2 c sun dried tomatoes, drained
1 15 oz can chickpeas, drained
Chili flakes to taste
1/2 lb fresh spinach
1 14 oz can coconut milk
1 tsp ground ginger
Freshly ground black pepper to taste
1/2 bunch cilantro, chopped

Drain and rinse the chickpeas and sun dried tomatoes. Sauté the onion over medium heat 3-4 minutes. Add a little water to deglaze pan. Add the garlic and fresh ginger and cook 1 minute. Add the sun dried tomatoes, lemon zest and chili flakes (optional) and cook 1 minute. Add the chickpeas and stir to coat. Turn up the heat and cook 3-4 minutes. Reduce the heat and slowly add the spinach a handful at a time. Add the coconut milk and bring to a simmer. Add the ground ginger, lemon juice, salt and pepper. Garnish with cilantro. Can be served over brown rice or grain of your choice.

Number of Servings: 4

Prep Time: 30 minutes

Personal Notes: Tridoshic but could be a main dish for Kapha individuals.

Ethiopian Wild Rice Pilaf (Tridoshic)

2 medium leeks, both parts, rinsed well and diced
2 cloves garlic, minced
3/4 tsp Berbere Spice Blend (Recipe in Sauces, Spice
  Mixes & Chutneys)
4 c cooked wild rice
15 oz can beans of your choice
Salt and pepper to taste
4 green onions, thinly sliced
Zest of 1 orange

Sauté leeks in a hot pan until slightly golden and translucent, about 4 minutes. Add a little water to deglaze the pan. Add garlic and cook for 2 minutes. Add the Berbere spice mix and cook 30 seconds. Stir in the wild rice, beans, orange zest and season with salt and pepper. Garnish with green onions.

Number of Servings: 4

Prep Time: 15 minutes

Personal Notes: Tridoshic but could be a main dish for Kapha individuals.

Green Bean Almondine

1 lb French green beans, trimmed
2 T unsalted butter
1/3 c raw sliced almonds
2 medium shallots, finely diced
2 medium garlic cloves, finely minced
1 small lemon, for zest and juice
Salt and black pepper

Add the green beans to a large pot of boiling water. Season generously with salt to ensure they will be seasoned inside and out and will retain their color. Blanch the beans for 4-5 minutes, until crisp-tender. Drain and set aside. In a skillet, melt the butter and add the sliced almonds. Sauté 2-3 minutes, stirring often until golden brown. Reduce heat, add the shallots and garlic, sauté 1-2 minutes. Add the green beans and sauté briefly, tossing them with the almonds. Add the lemon zest and lemon juice, toss again and season with salt and pepper. Serve immediately.

Number of Servings: 4

Prep Time: 15 minutes

Personal Notes: Great side dish for Pitta and Kapha Individuals.

Grilled Veggie Kabobs with Citrus Vinaigrette (Tridoshic)

2 c of your favorite vegetables, cut into pieces that can
 be skewered

Citrus Vinaigrette:
1/4 c olive oil
2 T lemon juice
Sea salt and ground black pepper

Make the vinaigrette, marinate the veggies in it for an hour, stirring to coat them. Make kabobs with 4 - 6 veggie pieces per skewer. Grill kabobs on a medium heat outdoor grill, turning halfway through and brushing with extra marinade. Cook until desired tenderness. Serve with rice and a protein of your choice.

Number of Servings: 4

Prep Time: 10 minutes plus cooking time

Personal Notes: Kapha can use vegetable broth in place of olive oil.

Lima Bean & Corn Salad (Tridoshic)

4 oz frozen baby lima beans
2 oz frozen yellow or white corn
2 oz frozen peas
1 onion, chopped
1/2 tsp garam masala
2 T fresh parsley, chopped
2 T fresh dill, chopped
1 T brown rice vinegar
1 T balsamic vinegar
1 T light rice vinegar
Dash of cayenne pepper
Salt and black pepper to taste

Thaw and cook the lima beans, corn and peas. Add all the veggies in a bowl and mix. Combine the rest of the ingredients together and pour over the veggies.

Number of Servings: 4

Prep Time: 15 minutes

Personal Notes: Tridoshic but could be a main dish for Kapha individuals.

Mango Lime Bean Salad (Tridoshic)

1 ripe mango, peeled and diced
1/2 red onion, diced
1 15 oz can cannelloni or great northern beans, drained
 and rinsed
1/2 c cilantro or parsley
1 lime, zest and juiced
1 c greens of your choice

Combine all but the greens and mix well. Serve over your favorite greens.

Number of Servings: 2

Prep Time: 10 minutes

Personal Notes: Tridoshic but could be a main dish for Kapha individuals.

Maple Roasted Spiced Carrots & Apples (Tridoshic)

1/4 c walnuts
3-4 carrots, thickly sliced
4-5 apples cut into thick wedges
1 1/2 T olive oil
1 1/2 tsp maple syrup
1/4 tsp cardamom, ground
1/4 tsp ginger, ground
1/4 tsp cinnamon, ground
2 tsp herbs, chopped, (sage & parsley or thyme & rosemary)
Salt to taste
1/4 of a lemon, juiced

Preheat oven to 425°. Toast walnuts in a skillet until fragrant. Set aside to cool, then finely chop. Line a baking pan with parchment paper. Toss carrots and apples with the olive oil and maple syrup. Sprinkle with spices and toss to coat evenly. Spread them in a single layer on the baking sheet and place in the upper part of the oven. Roast for 20 minutes and then gently flip them. Continue to bake until they are fork tender. When done, sprinkle with lemon juice, toss with fresh herbs and walnuts and season with salt. Serve immediately as a side dish, for breakfast or chill and serve with a salad.

Number of Servings: 3

Prep Time: 10 minutes plus cook time

Personal Notes: Kapha individuals should omit olive oil.

Mashed Cauliflower with Roasted Garlic

1 large head cauliflower, chopped into florets
3 T unsweetened almond milk
1 head garlic, roasted
1 T coconut oil
1/2 T nutritional yeast
1/4 tsp salt
Dash black pepper
Chopped herbs of your choice
2 c water

Preheat oven to 425°. Slice the top off the garlic head and place it sliced side up on a piece of foil large enough to wrap it up. Drizzle with coconut oil, wrap the foil around the garlic and place it on a baking sheet. Bake 30-35 minutes, or until tender. When the garlic is cool, peel the cloves off and squeeze the garlic out of each clove. Boil the water, add salt and the cauliflower. Cover and cook over medium heat 10-12 minutes or until tender. Drain cauliflower and put it in a blender with the milk, garlic, nutritional yeast and pepper. Blend until desired consistency. Add a tablespoon of your favorite chopped herbs to each serving. Try this with our Vegan Gravy (Recipe in Sauces, Spice Mixes & Chutneys).

Number of Servings: 4

Prep Time: 15 minutes plus cook times

Personal Notes: Great dish for Pitta and Kapha individuals.

Okra (Tridoshic)

1 c okra, washed and sliced, stems removed
1/2 tsp Ghee
1/4 tsp cumin
1/2 tsp coriander
Dash of dried mango powder
1 tsp fresh ginger, grated
1/2 tsp turmeric
Sea salt to taste

Heat Ghee and add fresh ginger, sauté 1 minute. Add all spices and cook for 2 minutes. Add the okra and cook 15 minutes or until it is tender. Add salt to taste.

Number of Servings: 2-3

Prep Time: 20 minutes

Personal Notes: Tridoshic but better for Vata individuals.

Orange Gingered Tofu

1 lb extra firm tofu
2 T fresh ginger, grated
3 garlic cloves, minced
3 T red onion, minced
1 c orange juice
1/4 c brown rice vinegar
1/4 c low sodium tamari
2 T toasted sesame seeds
1/4 tsp crushed red pepper flakes

Preheat oven to 350°. Wrap the tofu in paper towels and weigh it down to remove liquids. Let sit for at least 15 minutes. Combine all the other ingredients in a shallow baking dish and whisk together. Slice the tofu into cubes and place in the baking dish. Let it marinate 30 minutes. Once it's marinated, bake for 30 minutes or until it's nicely browned, turning once during the baking. This tofu can be served hot or cold, on top of a salad or separately as a side dish.

Number of Servings: 4

Prep Time: 35 minutes

Personal Notes: Great dish for Vata and Pitta individuals.

Potato Salad with Yogurt, Arugula and Dill

1 1/2 lbs new potatoes, cleaned, cut into quarters
1/2 c plain vegan yogurt
1/4 c vegan mayonnaise
2 large shallots, peeled and sliced thinly
1 bunch arugula, roughly chopped
1 small bunch fresh dill, finely chopped
Salt and black pepper to taste

Fill a 4 quart pot with water and salt generously. Bring to a boil and add the potatoes. Reduce heat and cook 15-20 minutes or until potatoes are tender. Drain. Whisk the yogurt and mayonnaise, toss with the potatoes. Add shallots, arugula and dill, season with salt and pepper.

Number of Servings: 4

Prep Time: 10 minutes plus cook time

Personal Notes: Best for Vata individuals.

Roasted Brussel Sprouts and Pears

1 lb Brussel sprouts, trimmed and sliced in half
1 Bosc pear, cored and sliced 1/4 inch thick lengthwise
1 large shallot, sliced thin
7 sprigs of thyme
1/4 tsp salt
1/8 tsp black pepper
2 T extra virgin olive oil
1 tsp fresh squeezed lemon juice
1/2 c hazelnuts or pecans, roughly chopped

Preheat oven to 425°, line a baking pan with parchment paper. Gently toss Brussel sprouts, pears, shallots, thyme, salt and pepper in olive oil and spread evenly on the baking pan. Roast 20-25 minutes, turning halfway through the cook time. The Brussel sprouts will be crispy and the pears will be slightly caramelized. Remove the thyme sprigs. Chop and toast the nuts in the same oven for the last 7 minutes of roasting. Drizzle the lemon juice over the sprouts and pears and toss with the nuts. Taste for any additional seasoning needed and garnish with extra thyme if desired.

Number of Servings: 4

Prep Time: 15 plus cook time

Personal Notes: Great dish for Pitta individuals. Kapha individuals can use vegetable broth in place of olive oil.

Roasted Fennel

1 fennel bulb
2 tsp Ghee

1/2 c brown rice or grain of your choice, cooked
1 c greens of your choice

Cucumber Mint Sauce (Recipe in Sauces, Spice Mixes &
  Chutneys)

Preheat oven to 350°. Cut fennel bulb in half and roast in oven for 20 minutes. Melt Ghee in a pan and sear the roasted fennel bulb in the hot pan on all sides. Serve with grains and greens of your choice. Top with the Cucumber Mint sauce.

Number of Servings: 4

Prep Time: 15 minutes plus cook times

Personal Notes: Great dish for Vata and Pitta individuals.

Spicy Roasted Cauliflower

1 large head cauliflower, cut into bite size pieces
1 lime, halved
1 tsp chili powder
1 tsp garlic powder
1 tsp oregano
1/2 tsp black pepper
2-3 T veggie stock or water
1/4 c fresh cilantro, chopped

Preheat oven to 450°. Put the cauliflower in a bowl and add the water or stock. Squeeze 1/2 the lime and toss to coat the cauliflower. Reserve the other 1/2 lime. Add the chili powder, garlic powder, oregano and pepper and toss to combine. Line a baking sheet with parchment paper and lay the cauliflower in a single layer. Include the other 1/2 of the lime with the cauliflower. Roast 15-20 minutes or until cooked to your liking. You may need to flip the veggies during cooking. To finish, re-squeeze lime halves over the cauliflower and season to taste. Top with fresh cilantro and serve.

Number of Servings: 3-4

Prep Time: 10 minutes plus baking time

Personal Notes: Great dish for Kapha individuals. Vata and Pitta individuals can have a small piece of it.

Stuffed Portobello Mushrooms (Tridoshic)

1/4 c quinoa
1/2 c veggie broth
1 tsp rosemary
1 tsp thyme
4 large portobello mushrooms, stems removed
1 T balsamic vinegar
1 T amino acids
1/2 tsp sea salt
1 c white beans, rinsed & drained
1 garlic clove, minced
1 T lemon juice
1/4 tsp black pepper
1 c baby spinach, finely chopped
1/4 c nutritional yeast

Preheat oven to 375°. Put quinoa in a saucepan with broth, rosemary and thyme. Bring to a boil, reduce heat and simmer, covered, for 10 minutes. Set aside and let sit until water is absorbed. Rub the mushrooms with amino acids and balsamic vinegar. Place cap side up on a baking pan covered with parchment paper. Sprinkle with sea salt, roast 5 minutes. Mash white beans in a bowl with a fork. Add garlic, lemon juice, salt and pepper to taste and stir until mixed. Add spinach, quinoa and nutritional yeast to the bean mixture, mix well. Stuff this mixture into the mushroom caps. Bake 15 minutes or until lightly browned. Serve immediately.

Number of Servings: 4

Prep Time: 20 minutes plus baking time

Personal Notes: Tridoshic but could be a main dish for Kapha individuals.

Tomato Salad with Red Onion, Dill and Feta

1/2 medium red onion, thinly sliced
1 lb tomatoes, preferably a mix of colors
2 T red wine vinegar
1 clove garlic, minced
Sea salt
1/4 c extra virgin olive oil
1 red bell pepper, seeded and cut into 1 inch pieces
1/3 medium English cucumber, thinly sliced
1 c Kalamata olives, pitted
1/4 c chopped fresh dill
1/4 c fresh mint leaves, coarsely chopped
1 c feta cheese, crumbled
Black pepper

Place the sliced onion in a bowl of cold water and set aside 10-15 minutes. Cut the tomatoes into bite sized chunks and put into a separate bowl. Whisk together the vinegar, garlic and salt in a large bowl. Drizzle in the olive oil and whisk to make the dressing. Drain the onion and pat dry. Add the onion, pepper, cucumber, dill and mint to the dressing. Mix well and let marinade for 10 minutes. Toss the tomatoes with the feta cheese, mix gently. Taste and season with salt and pepper. Top the tomato salad with the dressing and serve immediately.

Number of Servings: 4

Prep Time: 20 minutes

Personal Notes: Great dish for Vata individuals.

Vegetable Pilaf (Tridoshic)

1/2 c Basmati rice or quinoa
1/4 c cauliflower, chopped into bite size pieces
1/4 c green beans, cut into bite size pieces
1/4 c carrots, diced
1/4 c beets, diced
1/2 tsp ginger, grated
1/2 tsp garam masala
1 c water
1 tsp cilantro, chopped or 1 tsp mint leaves
1/2 tsp fresh lime juice
1/2 T Ghee
1/2 tsp salt

Heat Ghee is a saucepan. When hot, add spices and ginger and sauté for 1-2 minutes on low heat. Add rice or quinoa and sauté 3-4 more minutes until well coated with spices and Ghee. Add the veggies and sauté another 5-10 minutes. Add water and salt. Bring to a boil, reduce heat to low, cover and cook until water is completely absorbed. Serve with lime juice squeezed on top and garnish with cilantro or mint. Top with your favorite chutney (Recipes in Sauces, Spice Mixes & Chutneys).

Number of Servings: 4

Prep Time: 20 minutes

Wild Rice Salad (Tridoshic)

3 c cooked wild rice
1/4 c onion, finely chopped
14 oz black beans, drained
1/2 c shredded carrots
1/4 c fresh basil, chopped
1 T fresh ginger, minced
1/2 tsp sea salt
Pinch of fresh ground black pepper
1 lime

Combine all ingredients except lime. Stir to mix well. Squeeze fresh lime juice over the salad and serve.

Number of Servings: 4

Prep Time: 10 minutes plus cook time for wild rice

DESSERTS & SNACKS

Almond Butter Cookies

1 1/2 c wheat flour
1/2 tsp sea salt
1/2 c maple syrup
1/2 c coconut oil
1 tsp vanilla
1 c almond butter

Preheat oven to 350°. In a large bowl, combine dry ingredients and set aside. With a mixer or food processor, blend syrup, oil, vanilla and almond butter. Add the wet & dry ingredients together and mix well. Shape dough into 1 inch balls. Place on an ungreased cookie sheet and flatten gently with a fork. Bake 13-15 minutes.

Number of Servings: 2 dozen cookies

Prep Time: 25-30 minutes

Personal Notes: Most desserts are for Vata and Pitta individuals but Kapha individuals may have 1 serving.

Ayurvedic Bliss Balls

1 1/2 c dates, chopped
2 T almonds
2 T nuts of your choice
2 T cashews
5 whole dry figs, chopped
1 T coconut (optional)
2 pods green cardamom OR 1/8 tsp cardamom powder
1/8 tsp cinnamon
1/2 tsp Ghee (optional)

Coating Mixture: 2 T coconut flakes, 2 T finely chopped nuts, 2 T cocoa powder

Roast nuts in a pan until lightly browned. Peel and grind cardamom pods if using those. Add the dates, figs, coconut, Ghee and cardamom in a food processor. Add roasted nuts and grind until sticky, dough mixture forms. Using 1 tablespoon for each, form into small balls. Roll balls in coating mixture and store in the refrigerator for up to a week.

Prep Time: 25 minutes

Personal Notes: Most desserts are for Vata and Pitta individuals but Kapha individuals may have 1 serving.

Carrot Cupcakes

Cake:
2 c gluten free flour
1/2 tsp cardamom
1/4 tsp baking soda
2 tsp baking powder
1/8 tsp sea salt
3/4 c non dairy milk, unsweetened
3/4 c pure maple syrup
1/2 c applesauce, unsweetened
1 tsp apple cider vinegar
1 c carrots, grated
1 T ground flax seeds

Frosting:
3/4 c cashews
2 c carrots, grated
1/2 c water
1/2 c pure maple syrup
Pinch of salt
2 T toasted, slivered almonds

Preheat oven to 350°. Spray or line cupcake tins. Whisk together flour, cardamom, baking soda, baking powder, salt, set aside. Whisk together milk, syrup, applesauce and vinegar. Stir carrots and flax seeds into milk mixture and mix well. Stir milk mixture into the flour. Pour batter into 12 muffin tins. Bake 25 minutes or until a toothpick comes out clean. Set aside to cool. Frosting: In a saucepan combine carrots and water. Cook, covered, over high heat, until the water evaporates, about 10 minutes. Lower heat and add the syrup. Cook uncovered, until the syrup glazes the carrots, about 2 minutes. Remove from heat and let cool. Put the carrots and syrup in a blender, add cashews and salt and blend until smooth. Transfer to a bowl, cover and chill. Once the cake and frosting are cooled, frost cupcakes and sprinkle with almonds. Store in the refrigerator.

Number of Servings: 12 cupcakes

Prep Time: 30 minutes plus cook time

Personal Notes: Most desserts are for Vata and Pitta individuals but Kapha individuals may have 1 serving.

Coconut Rice Kheer

1/4 c basmati rice
1 c water
1 c coconut milk
2 T sweetener (maple syrup or pure cane sugar)
1/8 tsp cardamom powder
5 chopped cashews
1/2 tsp Ghee

Wash rice, add water and bring to a boil. Simmer until rice is soft. Add coconut milk and sweetener. Simmer until rice is very soft, remove from heat. Stir in cardamom powder. In a separate pan, heat the Ghee, add cashews and cook until golden brown. Chop and mix cashews into rice mixture. Chill 2 hours in individual cups.

Number of Servings: 3-4

Prep Time: 20 minutes

Personal Notes: Most desserts are for Vata and Pitta individuals but Kapha individuals may have 1 serving.

Nuts & Turmeric Granola

1/4 c and 2 T cashew paste
1 1/2 c old fashion oats
3/4 c cashews or walnuts
2 T sesame seeds
2 T flax seeds
1 tsp turmeric
1 tsp cinnamon
1/4 tsp grated nutmeg
1/2 tsp Himalayan salt
1/3 c maple syrup
1/3 c coconut oil
2 tsp vanilla
1/3 c cocoa nibs

Preheat oven to 350º. Line a baking sheet with parchment paper. Pulse the oats in a blender until moderately fine with a few chunks. Put the oats and nuts in a bowl and add sesame and flax seeds, turmeric, cinnamon, salt and nutmeg. In another bowl, whisk the syrup, coconut oil, cashew paste and vanilla. Pour the liquid over the oat mixture and mix well. Spoon this onto the baking sheet and spread it into a single layer. Press it together so it bakes into a granola type crunchiness. Bake 20-25 minutes, until the edges are golden brown. Halfway through, flip it so the granola browns on both sides. Let it cool, then break into pieces and toss with cocoa nibs. Store at room temperature.

Number of Servings: 2 cups

Prep Time: 45 minutes

Personal Notes: These are okay for Vata and Pitta individuals but Kapha may have 1 serving.

Pistachio Tapioca Kheer

1 1/2 c coconut milk
1 c tapioca
1/2 c sugar
Pinch of salt
1/4 tsp ginger powder
1/8 tsp cardamom
1/8 tsp nutmeg
2 T raisins
2 T ground pistachios
2 T ground almonds

Cook tapioca and sugar in the coconut milk with a pinch of salt. Bring to a boil then turn heat down and simmer for 5 minutes. Dry roast the pistachios and almonds in the oven for a few minutes. Add the ginger, cardamom, nutmeg and raisins to the tapioca milk. Simmer until it thickens. Serve chilled.

Number of Servings: 3

Prep Time: 25 minutes

Personal Notes: Most desserts are for Vata and Pitta individuals but Kapha individuals may have 1 serving.

Rolled Oats Granola Trail Mix (Tridoshic)

2 c rolled oats
4 T chia seeds
4 T flax meal
4 T hemp seeds
2 tsp cinnamon
1/2 tsp clove powder
1/2 tsp cardamom seeds
Dash of Hing
1/2 tsp black pepper
1/4 tsp ginger powder
2 T Ghee
Berries and seeds optional for toppings

Preheat oven to 400º. Mix all ingredients in a bowl. Line a baking pan with parchment paper and spread the mixture in a layer. Bake 20 minutes. If desired, top with 1/4 c cranberries or raisins, 1/4 c pumpkin or sunflower seeds and bake another 10 minutes. Use as a snack.

Number of Servings: 2 cups

Prep Time: 30 minutes

Vegan Rice Pudding

1/2 c basmati rice, cooked about 11 minutes
2 1/2 to 3 c almond milk
3 1/2 T cashews
2 pods of cardamom
Pinch of salt
1/4 c sugar
2 1/2 T raisins
2 1/2 T chopped nuts of your choice

Blend almond milk with cashews in a blender until smooth. After rice has cooked down, add the milk mixture to the rice. Put the rice mixture in a skillet and add the sugar, salt, cardamom seeds and simmer for 15-20 minutes. In a separate pan, toast the nuts until golden brown and set aside. Add the raisins to the rice mixture and cook for 1 minute. Taste and adjust sweetness to your likeness. Continue to simmer until the rice is tender and has thickened, about 15 minutes. Serve warm or chilled, garnish with toasted nuts.

Number of Servings: 2

Prep Time: 15 minutes plus cook time

Personal Notes: Most desserts are for Vata and Pitta individuals but Kapha individuals may have 1 serving.

CHUTNEYS, DRESSINGS & SAUCES

Chutney: Fresh Coriander (Tridoshic)

1 bunch fresh coriander OR cilantro OR Chinese parsley,
  chopped
1/4 c fresh lemon juice
1/4 c water
1/4 c grated coconut
2 T fresh ginger, chopped
1 tsp honey
1 tsp sea salt

In a blender, pulse the lemon juice, water and fresh coriander, until it is smooth. Add the rest of the ingredients and blend until it is paste-like. Use this sauce on roasted root vegetables or the chickpea pancakes.

Number of Servings: 3/4 cup

Prep Time: 10 minutes

Personal Notes: All chutneys, and sauces are Tridoshic but excess will increase Pitta.

Chutney: Mint Coconut (Tridoshic)

1 c fresh mint leaves, loosely packed
2 T grated coconut
1 tsp Ghee
1 T sesame seeds
1/2 tsp sea salt
1/2 c water
1 T lemon juice

Heat Ghee in a sauce pan. Add sesame seeds and sauté lightly. Add mint leaves and coconut, cover and simmer 5-7 minutes. Add water and salt, simmer 5 minutes. After cooling, add lemon juice. Purée in a blender until smooth.

Number of Servings: 1 cup

Prep Time: 15 minutes

Personal Notes: All chutneys, and sauces are Tridoshic but excess will increase Pitta.

Dressing: Anti-inflammatory Turmeric (Tridoshic)

1 avocado, halved and pitted
2 T lemon juice
1 tsp lemon zest
4 garlic cloves
1 T turmeric powder
2 T raw honey
1/2 tsp Himalayan Salt
2 T coconut oil
1/2 inch ginger, peeled

Process all ingredients in a blender until smooth. This dressing can be used on greens or on cooked vegetables.

Number of Servings: 1/2 cup

Prep Time: 10 minutes

Dressing: Asian Dressing

3 T rice vinegar
2 tsp miso
1 1/2 T maple syrup
2 T soy sauce or tamari
1 tsp sriracha sauce (to taste)
1 1/2 T fresh ginger, minced
2 cloves garlic, minced
1 T toasted sesame oil

Whisk all ingredients together and use over salad greens or with Asian Wild Rice Salad recipe (Recipe in Side Dishes).

Number of Servings: 1/2 cup

Prep Time: 10 minutes

Personal Notes: Great for Vata individuals. Pitta and Kapha individuals should use very small quantity.

Dressing: Avocado Ranch (Tridoshic)

1 to 1 1/2 c non-dairy milk
1 avocado, pitted
2 T nutritional yeast
1-2 cloves of garlic
1 T onion powder
1/4 tsp chipotle powder
1/4 tsp black pepper
Sea salt to taste
2 T fresh dill, minced
1 tsp Dijon mustard
1 lemon, juiced (optional for taste)
3 T chives, minced

Add all ingredients except chives to a blender. Blend until smooth. If using as a dressing, use 1 cup of milk to start and then add as needed for desired consistency. The dressing should be thick but pourable. Add salt, pepper, lemon juice and chipotle powder to taste. Top with chives before serving.

Number of Servings: 2 cups

Prep Time: 15 minutes

Dressing: Cashew Caesar (Tridoshic)

1/2 c raw cashews
2-3 c warm water

1/2 c unsweetened almond milk
2 1/2 T white wine vinegar
1 garlic clove, peeled
1 1/2 T kelp or seaweed
1 T natural sweetener, such as agave or honey
1 T light soy or chickpea miso
2 T Dijon mustard
1/2 tsp fresh ground pepper
1/2 lemon, juiced

Soak the cashews in warm water for 3-4 hours until soft, then strain them. Place all ingredients in a blender and mix until desired consistency. Use as a salad dressing.

Number of Servings: 2 cups

Prep Time: 10 minutes plus soaking time for cashews

Dressing: Dijon Lemon Tahini (Tridoshic)

3 T shallots or onion, minced
3 T Dijon mustard
2 T tahini paste
4 T lemon juice
2 T nutritional yeast
1/2 tsp garlic granules
1/2 tsp onion granules
Sea salt to taste
Ground black pepper to taste
1/4 - 1/2 c water

Add all ingredients to the blender, starting with 1/4 cup water. Blend until smooth and add more water for desired consistency. Keep in the refrigerator up to 4 days.

Number of Servings: 1 cup

Prep Time: 10 minutes

Dressing: Dijon Vinagrette

1/4 c Dijon mustard
1/2 c rice vinegar
1/4 c nut paste
1 1/2 tsp sweetener such as agave or honey
1 1/2 T shallot, minced
1/4 tsp ground black pepper
1 clove garlic, minced
1 T tarragon
Water or orange juice as needed

Whisk all ingredients together. Add water or orange juice as needed for desired consistency. Use as a salad dressing or pour over cooked vegetables.

Number of Servings: 1 1/4 cups

Prep Time: 15 minutes

Personal Notes: Great for Vata individuals. Pitta and Kapha individuals should use very small quantity.

Dressing: Lemon Mango

1 c extra virgin olive oil
1/2 c mango pulp
1/2 c fresh lemon juice
1/2 tsp dill, chopped
1/2 tsp Himalayan salt

Whisk all ingredients together. Let sit for 2 hours before serving over salad.

Number of Servings: 2

Prep Time: 10 minutes plus marinating time

Personal Notes: Great for Vata individuals. Pitta and Kapha individuals should use very small quantity.

Dressing: Mustard Ginger (Tridoshic)

1/2 c extra virgin olive oil
2 T lemon juice
1/2 tsp honey
1 tsp fresh turmeric, grated
1 tsp fresh ginger, grated
1 T cilantro, chopped finely
Pinch black pepper and sea salt
1/2 tsp Dijon mustard
1/2 tsp cumin
1/2 tsp coriander
1/2 tsp fennel powder
1 tsp coconut amino acids

Mix all ingredients well with a whisk. Use over salad greens.

Number of Servings: 2

Prep Time: 10 minutes

Personal Notes:

Dressing: Orange Ginger

4 T orange juice
1 tsp ginger, grated
4 tsp extra virgin olive oil
1 tsp fresh oregano, chopped
2 cloves garlic, minced
1 tsp lemon zest
1 T honey
1/4 tsp Himalayan salt
1/4 tsp ground black pepper

Put all ingredients in a blender and mix until desired consistency. Use over salad greens.

Number of Servings: 1

Prep Time: 10 minutes

Personal Notes: Great for Vata individuals. Pitta and Kapha individuals should use very small quantity.

Dressing: Rainbow (Tridoshic)

2 T almond butter
2 T lemon juice
1 T rice vinegar
1/3 c water
2 tsp maple syrup
2 tsp ground chia seeds
Dash salt & pepper

Combine all ingredients in a blender and mix until smooth. Let sit for 5 minutes before using.

Number of Servings: 2

Prep Time: 10 minutes

Dressing: Spicy Chipotle

1 c unsweetened non-dairy milk
1 T chia seeds or ground flax seeds
2 T fresh lemon juice
1 T apple cider vinegar
1 date or 1 tsp sweetener of your choice
1 small clove of garlic
1 tsp miso paste
3 sun-dried tomatoes (not in oil) or 2 tsp tomato paste
1/4 to 1/2 tsp chipotle powder, based on taste
1/4 tsp ground cumin
Water, as needed

Pour the milk into a blender then add the rest of the ingredients. Blend until smooth and let it sit for 15 minutes to thicken. To use as a dressing, add a bit of water until desired consistency. To use as a dip for chips or veggies, let it thicken first. Store in refrigerator.

Number of Servings: 1 1/2 cups

Prep Time: 15 minutes

Personal Notes: Great for Vata individuals. Pitta and Kapha individuals should use very small quantity.

Dressing: Sunshine (Tridoshic)

2 1/2 T cashew or other nut base paste
1/2 tsp turmeric
1/2 tsp curry powder
1/2 T Dijon mustard
1 garlic clove
2 T apple cider vinegar
1 carrot, cut into chunks
1/2 c oil
1 tsp honey
1 tsp sea salt
1/2 tsp fresh ground black pepper
2 T water
Pinch of red pepper flakes (optional)

Put all ingredients except for the oil and water into a blender. Blend, slowly adding the oil. Adjust the seasonings to taste and add the water until desired consistency.

Number of Servings: 1 cup

Prep Time: 10 minutes

Dressing: Sweet Balsamic (Tridoshic)

1/2 c good quality balsamic vinegar
3 T low sodium tamari
3 T maple syrup
1/2 T onion, minced
1 clove garlic, finely minced
1 1/2 T nutritional yeast (optional)
1 T fresh herbs of your choice, minced (chives, oregano, rosemary)
Ground black pepper to taste

In a small bowl, whisk together all ingredients or place in a jar and shake vigorously. Use as a salad dressing or over cooked potatoes and sliced peppers as a side dish. Can also be used as a marinade for mushrooms before grilling.

Number of Servings: 1 cup

Prep Time: 15 minutes

Dressing: Vegan Poppy Seed

2 T tahini
1 T apple cider vinegar
1/4 c extra virgin olive oil
1/4 c grated onion
1 tsp salt
1/2 tsp black pepper
2 tsp sugar
1 T poppy seeds

Combine all dressing ingredients in a bowl and whisk until smooth.

Number of Servings: 2

Prep Time: 5 minutes

Personal Notes: Great for Vata individuals. Pitta and Kapha individuals should use very small quantity.

Dressing: Vegan Ranch

1/2 c nut paste of your choice
2/3 c full fat coconut milk
2 T fresh lemon juice
1/2 tsp garlic powder
1/2 tsp sea salt
1/4 tsp ground black pepper
1/2 tsp dried or fresh dill, chopped
1 tsp fresh chives

Add nut base, dry seasonings and spices to a blender. Add coconut milk and lemon juice and blend until smooth. Stir in fresh herbs by hand. Use as a dressing or a dip.

Number of Servings: 1 1/4 cup of dressing

Prep Time: 10 minutes

Personal Notes: Great for Vata and Pitta individuals. Kapha individuals should use very small quantity.

Sauce: Basic Ayurvedic Vagar (Tridoshic)

1 large onion, diced
2 carrot, diced
2 celery stalks, diced
1 T Ghee
4 garlic cloves, diced
1 inch fresh ginger, grated
2 tsp cumin seeds
2 tsp coriander
Sea salt to taste
1 tsp mango powder
2 tsp turmeric powder
1/4 tsp black cumin seeds
Dash of Hing
1/4 tsp celery seeds
1 tsp garam masala
1/4 c water or veggie broth

Dry sauté onion in skillet 2-3 minutes. Add Ghee, then the garlic, ginger, cumin, Hing, coriander, mango powder, turmeric, black cumin, celery seeds and garam masala. Sauté 1 minute and then add water or broth. Add carrots and celery and cook another 10 minutes. Add salt to taste.

Number of Servings: About 1 cup

Prep Time: 15 minutes

Personal Notes: Use this as a soup or kitchari base or serve it over your favorite cooked vegetables.

Sauce: Cucumber Mint (Tridoshic)

1/2 cucumber, peeled and diced
4-5 sprigs fresh mint
3 T olive oil
1 1/2 lime or lemon, juiced
Salt and pepper to taste

Put all ingredients in a blender and pulse until desired consistency. Use with spicy veggies to cool them down.

Number of Servings: 1

Prep Time: 10 minutes

Personal Notes: All chutneys, and sauces are Tridoshic. This recipe can be Pitta pacifying.

Sauce: Oil Free Marinara (Tridoshic)

1 28 oz can crushed tomatoes
1 T dried oregano
1 T dried basil
1 tsp onion powder
3/4 tsp garlic powder
Dash red pepper flakes
1 T maple syrup
Sea salt to taste

Place all ingredients in a large pot and simmer over medium to medium-high heat for 2-3 minutes. Reduce heat to low and cook another 5-6 minutes, stirring frequently. Serve over pasta or use as a pizza sauce.

Number of Servings: 2 cups

Prep Time: 15 minutes

Personal Notes: All chutneys, and sauces are Tridoshic but excess will increase Pitta.

Sauce: Vegan Pesto (Tridoshic)

2 c packed fresh basil, large stems removed
3 T pine nuts or walnuts
3 cloves garlic
2 T lemon juice
3-4 T nutritional yeast
1/4 tsp sea salt
2-3 T extra virgin olive oil or vegetable broth
3-6 T water

Add all ingredients except olive oil to a blender. Blend on high until a paste forms. Add olive oil a little at a time while blender runs. Add water slowly until desired consistency. The sauce should be thick but pourable. Taste and adjust seasonings as needed. Use on veggies for a side dish or pour over pasta. Add to sauces or dressings for flavor. Store in refrigerator for up to a week or pour into ice cube trays and freeze for up to a month. Take out cubes and use in dishes as needed.

Number of Servings: 1 cup

Prep Time: 15 minutes

Personal Notes: All chutneys, and sauces are Tridoshic but excess will increase Pitta.

Sauce: Vegan Gravy

4 T coconut oil
1 medium onion, diced
1/4 c all purpose flour
3/4 c no-sodium veggie broth
2 T soy sauce
1 T vegan Worcestershire sauce
1 tsp poultry seasoning
Salt and pepper to taste

Heat coconut oil in medium saucepan. Add onion and cook until translucent. Whisk in the flour, making a roux. Slowly whisk in veggie broth, a little at a time. Add soy and Worcestershire sauce, whisking until thickened, simmer 15 minutes. Add salt & pepper to taste. Use over Lentil Loaf or Mashed Cauliflower.

Number of Servings: 4

Prep Time: 15 minutes

Personal Notes: Excellent for Vata and Pitta individuals.

DIPS & DRINKS

Dip: Creamy Spinach Artichoke (Tridoshic)

1 jar marinated artichoke hearts, drained
2 c raw spinach, chopped
1/4 c water
2 T almond paste
Pinch of salt and pepper

Place all ingredients in a blender and pulse until everything is well blended. Can be served warm or at room temperature. Serve with veggies or chips.

Number of Servings: 2

Prep Time: 10 minutes

Personal Notes: Tridoshic but better for Pitta individuals in hot weather.

Dip: Fresh Tomato Salsa (Tridoshic)

3 Roma tomatoes, diced
1 small red onion, diced
1 garlic clove, minced
1 small jalapeño pepper, diced
1 1/2 tsp lime juice
1/2 tsp Himalayan Salt
1/2 tsp raw sugar
1/2 tsp cumin powder
1/8 c fresh cilantro, minced

Stir all ingredients in a large bowl. For a smoother salsa, use your blender to get to your desired consistency. Chill for 30 minutes and serve with raw veggies such as carrots, bell pepper slices or Tortilla chips.

Number of Servings: 4

Prep Time: 10 minutes

Personal Notes: Tridoshic but excess will increase Pitta. Pitta individuals should avoid Jalapeño pepper.

Dip: Hummus (Tridoshic)

½ c chickpeas (or 1/4 c chickpeas & 1/4 c navy or black
  beans), soaked, drained, rinsed, boiled until soft
1/4 tsp Hing
6 inches seaweed
4 cloves garlic, minced
1/2 in ginger, grated
1/2 tsp Himalayan salt
1 tsp cumin seeds
1/2 tsp garam masala
2 lemons or 2 limes, juiced
2 T tahini paste
2 T water from soaked beans

Put all ingredients into a blender and mix until desired
consistency. Add more water from the beans if needed to
get the right consistency. Use as a dressing for Bowl
recipes or with chips or veggies for a snack.

Number of Servings: 1/2 cup

Prep Time: 15 minutes

Dip: Vegan French Onion Dip

1 medium onion, diced
1 T olive oil
1 tsp Worcestershire sauce
1/4 tsp garlic powder
1/4 tsp onion powder
Sea salt to taste

"Sour cream" sauce:
1/3 c water
1/2 c nut paste
1 T lemon juice
1 tsp apple cider vinegar
1/2 tsp sea salt

Make the "Sour Cream" sauce by putting those ingredients into a blender on medium high for 30 seconds. Refrigerate to thicken. Heat oil in a skillet and add the diced onion. Sauté, stirring frequently for 25-30 minutes until caramelized. Cover the pan intermittently or add water if the onions are drying out. Set aside to cool. In a small bowl, mix the "Sour Cream" sauce, garlic and onion powders, Worcestershire and salt. Fold the onions into this mix. Garnish with parsley if desired. Serve with chips, crackers or veggies.

Number of Servings: 1 cup

Prep Time: 20 minutes

Personal Notes: Great for Vata individuals.

Dip: Vegan Queso (Tridoshic)

1/4 c plus 2 T nut paste
1/4 c water
1/3 c roasted peppers, drained
1/4 c nutritional yeast
2 T lemon juice
2 garlic cloves
1 medium scallion or large slice of red onion, chopped
1 T olive oil
2 tsp smoked paprika or chipotle powder
1 tsp cumin
Pinch of cayenne pepper
Salt to taste

Place water in a blender and then add the rest of the ingredients. Blend on high about 30 seconds or until very smooth and creamy. Taste and adjust seasonings as needed. Use as a dip, or over warm black beans or as a sauce for tacos.

Number of Servings: 1 cup dressing

Prep Time: 15 minutes

Drink: Golden Milk

1 tsp fresh turmeric, diced
1/2 tsp coconut oil
1/4 tsp black pepper
1 c almond or cashew or coconut milk
1 tsp honey or 1 1/2 tsp of agave
Dash of cinnamon, cloves, cardamom

Combine first 3 ingredients in a small saucepan. Warm over low heat, stirring continuously. Remove from heat and strain. Add milk and warm up again. Sprinkle with a dash of cinnamon, cloves and cardamom. Whisk together, remove from heat and add honey or agave before serving.

Number of Servings: 1

Prep Time: 10 minutes

Personal Notes: Great for Vata and Pitta individuals.

Drink: Herbal Energy (Tridoshic)

5 c water
2 T ginger, chopped
1 1/2 tsp green tea
1 1/2 tsp Stevia sweetener
1/2 tsp cinnamon
1 bunch parsley
1 lemon or lime
2 T honey

In a saucepan, bring water, ginger, green tea, Stevia, cinnamon, and parsley to a boil. Take off heat, cover and let steep for 10 minutes. Add juice of 1 lemon or lime and honey. Store in a thermos and drink for energy boost.

Number of Servings: 4

Prep Time: 15 minutes

Personal Notes: Could also use any fresh dry herbs and spices such as dill, turmeric, cilantro, basil, mint, lemongrass, thyme, rosemary, orange peels, cardamom, black pepper and dates. Experiment and enjoy everyday!

Drink: Vegan Chai Spiced Eggnog

2 c unsweetened almond milk
1 can coconut milk
1 tsp grated nutmeg
3 cinnamon sticks
1/2 tsp ground ginger or 3 inch fresh ginger, grated
15 black peppercorns
6 pods cardamom, smashed
1 star anise (optional)
1/8 tsp turmeric
6-7 pitted dates
2 tsp vanilla
1/8 tsp Himalayan salt

In a medium saucepan, over medium-low heat, cook almond milk, coconut milk, nutmeg, cinnamon, ginger, peppercorns, cardamom, anise and turmeric. Bring to a simmer and remove from heat. Stir, cover and let steep for 20 minutes. Strain over a blender and discard solids. Add dates, vanilla and salt to the blender. Blend until completely smooth,1-2 minutes. Pour into a container and chill until ready to serve. It will thicken as it cools. Serve cold or warm, with or without a splash of rum or use as a coffee creamer. Sprinkle with a little nutmeg. Keeps for 3-4 days.

Number of Servings: 4

Prep Time: 30 minutes

Personal Notes: Great for Vata and Pitta individuals.

Drink: CCF Tea (Tridoshic)

1 tsp coriander
1 tsp cumin
1 tsp fennel powder
4 c water

Put all ingredients in a pan, bring to a boil and simmer 10 minutes.

Number of Servings: 4

Prep Time: 10 minutes

Personal Notes: Add 1 tsp turmeric powder if immunity is needed. Add 1/4 tsp Ajwain seeds is flatulence is present. Good for digestion and acidity.

Drink: Fenugreek Tea

4 c water
1 T fenugreek

Place all ingredients in a pot, bring to a boil and simmer 10 minutes.

Number of Servings: 4

Prep Time: 10 minutes

Personal Notes: Good for detoxification. Pitta pacifying.

SPICE MIXES

Spice Mix: Ethiopian Berbere

1/2 c ground, diced chilis
1/4 c paprika
1 T cayenne pepper
1 tsp onion powder
1 tsp ground ginger
1 tsp cumin
1 tsp ground coriander
1 tsp ground cardamom
1 tsp ground fenugreek
1/2 tsp garlic powder
1/2 tsp ground cinnamon
1/4 tsp ground nutmeg
1/2 tsp ground allspice
1/2 tsp ground cloves

Mix all ingredients together well. Store in an air-tight container. This Ethiopian spice mixture can be used for seasoning stews, soups, grains or veggies.

Prep Time: 10 minutes

Personal Notes: This is very spicy and a true taste of Ethiopia. You can also buy it pre-made. Pitta should use sparingly.

Spice Mix: Pitta Spice Mix

2 T fennel seeds
2 T coriander seeds
1 T cumin seeds
1/2 T cardamom seeds
2 T turmeric powder
1 T ginger powder
1/2 tsp cinnamon
1 T fenugreek
1 T Himalayan salt
1/2 T black pepper
1 T sugar cane

Dry sauté all seeds for 2 minutes. Cool, then grind them in a coffee/spice grinder. Add the rest of the ingredients, mix well and store in an airtight container.

Number of Servings: 12

Prep Time: 10 minutes

Personal Notes: This seasoning mix can be used when eating out or at home over meats, soups, etc., to enhance Agni. Use 1 tablespoon per person in your recipes. Pitta pacifying.

Spice Mix: Chaat Masala (Tridoshic)

3 T cumin seeds
1 T coriander seeds
1 1/2 tsp fennel seeds (saunf)
1/4 c dried mango powder (amchur powder)
3 T kosher salt
1 1/2 tsp freshly ground black pepper
1 1/2 tsp ground ginger
1 1/2 tsp ajwain seeds (celery seeds)
1 tsp dried mint
1/4 tsp Hing

Dry roast the seeds for 2-3 minutes in a skillet. Grind in a coffee/spice grinder. Mix with the powders and store in an airtight container.

Number of Servings: 1/2 cup spice mix

Prep Time: 5 minutes

Personal Notes: This spice mix is Tridoshic but excess will increase Pitta.

Spice Mix: Chai Masala (Tridoshic)

2 T black peppercorns
2 T whole cardamom
4 cinnamon sticks
2 T ginger powder
1 T whole cloves
4 star anise

Grind everything but the ginger powder in a coffee/spice grinder for 1 minute. Add ginger powder and mix well. Store in an airtight container. Use 1 teaspoon of Chai Masala and 2 teaspoons of black tea leaves for 4 cups of chai tea.

Number of Servings: 20

Prep Time: 10 minutes

Personal Notes: Tridoshic but best for Kapha individuals.

Spice Mix: Kapha Spice Mix

2 T mustard seeds
2 T cumin seeds
2 T coriander seeds
1 T anise seeds
1 T fenugreek seeds
1/2 T cardamom seeds
1 T ginger powder
2 T turmeric powder
1/2 T cinnamon
1 T Himalayan salt
1 T black pepper

Dry sauté all seeds for 2 minutes. Cool and grind in a coffee/spice grinder. Add powders and mix well. Store in an airtight container.

Number of Servings: 12

Prep Time: 10 minutes

Personal Notes: This seasoning mix can be used when eating out or at home over meats, soups, etc., to enhance Agni. Use 1 tablespoon of spice mix per person in your recipes. Kapha pacifying.

Spice Mix: Tridoshic Mix

2 tsp cumin seeds
2 tsp coriander seeds
1 tsp celery seeds
2 tsp fennel seeds
1/2 tsp fenugreek seeds
1 tsp mustard seeds (1 teaspoon more in winter)
2 tsp dried mango powder
2 tsp turmeric
1 tsp garam masala
1 tsp black pepper
2 tsp Himalayan salt
1/2 tsp Hing

In a skillet, dry sauté all seeds for 2 minutes. After they're cooled, grind them in a coffee/spice grinder. Mix the seeds with the powders. Store in an airtight container.

Number of Servings: 1/2 cup spice mix

Prep Time: 5 minutes

Personal Notes: This seasoning mix can be used when eating out or at home over meats, soups, etc., to enhance Agni. Use 1 tablespoon per person in your recipes.

Spice Mix: Vata Spice Mix

4 T cumin seeds
1 T fenugreek seeds
1 T Ajwain (celery seed)
2 T turmeric powder
1 T ginger powder
2 T Himalayan salt
1 T sugar cane
1 T black pepper
1/4 tsp Hing

Dry sauté all seeds for 2 minutes. Cool and grind in a coffee/spice grinder. Mix in the rest of the ingredients. Store in an airtight container.

Number of Servings: 12

Prep Time: 5 minutes

Personal Notes: This seasoning mix can be used when eating out or at home over meats, soups, etc., to enhance Agni. Use 1 tablespoon of this spice mix per person in your recipes. Vata pacifying.

Notes

Notes

Index of Recipes

Index of Recipes by Category

Smashed Chickpea Salad Sandwich (Tridoshic) *66*
Spicy Asian Tacos *67*
Thai Curry with Tofu *68*
Vegan Chili Spinach Pie *70*
Vegan Tacos with Corn Slaw *71*
Vegan Vegetable Lasagna (Tridoshic) *73*

SIDE DISHES
Asian Wild Rice Salad (Tridoshic) *76*
Barley Sauté (Tridoshic) *77*
Chickpeas with Spinach & Sun Dried Tomatoes (Tridoshic) *78*
Ethiopian Wild Rice Pilaf (Tridoshic) *79*
Green Bean Almondine *80*
Grilled Veggie Kabobs with Citrus Vinaigrette (Tridoshic) *81*
Lima Bean & Corn Salad (Tridoshic) *82*
Mango Lime Bean Salad (Tridoshic) *83*
Maple Roasted Spiced Carrots & Apples (Tridoshic) *84*
Mashed Cauliflower with Roasted Garlic *85*
Okra (Tridoshic) *86*
Orange Gingered Tofu *87*
Potato Salad with Yogurt, Arugula and Dill *88*
Roasted Brussel Sprouts and Pears *89*
Roasted Fennel *90*
Spicy Roasted Cauliflower *91*
Stuffed Portobello Mushrooms (Tridoshic) *92*
Tomato Salad with Red Onion, Dill and Feta *93*
Vegetable Pilaf (Tridoshic) *94*
Wild Rice Salad (Tridoshic) *95*

DESSERTS & SNACKS
Almond Butter Cookies *98*
Ayurvedic Bliss Balls *99*
Carrot Cupcakes *100*
Coconut Rice Kheer *102*
Nuts & Turmeric Granola *103*
Pistachio Tapioca Kheer *104*
Rolled Oats Granola Trail Mix (Tridoshic) *105*
Vegan Rice Pudding *106*

CHUTNEYS, DRESSINGS & SAUCES
Chutney: Fresh Coriander (Tridoshic) *108*
Chutney: Mint Coconut (Tridoshic) *109*
Dressing: Anti-inflammatory Turmeric (Tridoshic) *110*
Dressing: Asian Dressing *111*
Dressing: Avocado Ranch (Tridoshic) *112*
Dressing: Cashew Caesar (Tridoshic) *113*
Dressing: Dijon Lemon Tahini (Tridoshic) *114*
Dressing: Dijon Vinagrette *115*
Dressing: Lemon Mango *116*
Dressing: Mustard Ginger (Tridoshic) *117*
Dressing: Orange Ginger *118*
Dressing: Rainbow (Tridoshic) *119*
Dressing: Spicy Chipotle *120*
Dressing: Sunshine (Tridoshic) *121*
Dressing: Sweet Balsamic (Tridoshic) *122*
Dressing: Vegan Poppy Seed *123*

Dressing: Vegan Ranch   *124*
Sauce: Basic Ayurvedic Vagar (Tridoshic)   *125*
Sauce: Cucumber Mint (Tridoshic)   *126*
Sauce: Oil Free Marinara (Tridoshic)   *127*
Sauce: Vegan Pesto (Tridoshic)   *128*
Sauce: Vegan Gravy   *129*

DIPS & DRINKS
Dip: Creamy Spinach Artichoke (Tridoshic)   *132*
Dip: Fresh Tomato Salsa (Tridoshic)   *133*
Dip: Hummus (Tridoshic)   *134*
Dip: Vegan French Onion Dip   *135*
Dip: Vegan Queso (Tridoshic)   *136*
Drink: Golden Milk   *137*
Drink: Herbal Energy (Tridoshic)   *138*
Drink: Vegan Chai Spiced Eggnog   *139*
Drink: CCF Tea (Tridoshic)   *140*
Drink: Fenugreek Tea   *141*

SPICE MIXES
Spice Mix: Ethiopian Berbere   *144*
Spice Mix: Pitta Spice Mix   *145*
Spice Mix: Chaat Masala (Tridoshic)   *146*
Spice Mix: Chai Masala (Tridoshic)   *147*
Spice Mix: Kapha Spice Mix   *148*
Spice Mix: Tridoshic Mix   *149*
Spice Mix: Vata Spice Mix   *150*

The Dosha Quiz to determine Mind Body Constitution

There are two parts to this questionnaire. The first part determines your unique constitution or Prakriti. Answer the questions in Part I based on how you have been all your life both on a physical as well as psychological basis. If one answer alone does not feel like an accurate description, then you can use two answers. When finished, add up all of the columns. The column with the highest sum denotes your constitution. The Second Part of the questionnaire helps to determine your current state of balance or Vikriti.

Part I

Frame	☐ I have small bones, am thin and slender with a slight build, fairly narrow hips and shoulders. Some would say I am unusually tall or short.	☐ I have medium bones, am asymmetrical, of average height, with a well-proportioned build.	☐ I have a sturdy, heavier build and am of average height.
Weight	☐ I have a tendency to lose weight.	☐ I find it easy to gain weight.	☐ I gain weight easily but have difficulty losing it.
Eyes	☐ My eyes are relatively small and some would say my gaze is active or curious.	☐ I have medium sized eyes and most would say I have a penetrating gaze.	☐ I have relatively large eyes and most would say my gaze is soft and pleasant.
Complexion	☐ My skin is dry, rough and thin. I tan easily without burning. I have few moles that are dark in color.	☐ My skin is warm and reddish. I burn easily in the sun. I have many brownish red moles and freckles.	☐ My skin is soft, thick, moist and smooth. I can tan after long exposure. I have a few light moles and some white blotches.
Hair	☐ My hair tends to be dry, brittle, scant and curly, sometimes frizzy. My eyelashes are thin.	☐ My hair is fine and straight, blond, red, or prematurely gray in color. I have a tendency toward baldness or thinning hair.	☐ My hair is soft, thick, and abundant.
Joints	☐ My joints are thin, prominent and tend to crack. My veins and tendons are noticeable.	☐ My joints are loose and flexible. My veins and tendons are prominent.	☐ My joints are large and padded. My veins and tendons are not prominent.
Menses (for women)	☐ My cycle is irregular. My flow is scant and dark.	☐ My cycle is regular and my flow is intense and red.	☐ My cycle is average and flow is light.
Appetite	☐ My appetite varies. I like to eat frequently though sometimes I forget to eat.	☐ I have a moderate to strong appetite. I like to have regular meals on time and don't like to miss meals.	☐ I like to eat but am often not really hungry. I can miss a meal with little effect.
Food Preferences	☐ I love salads and crunchy snacks.	☐ I love spicy, hot, oily foods.	☐ I enjoy sweet, starchy foods.

Sex Drive	☐ I am easily aroused and quickly satiated.	☐ I can be romantic and passionate with a strong sex drive, controlled passion and average stamina.	☐ I am slow to be aroused, but am deeply involved and have good stamina.
Sleep Pattern	☐ I am a light sleeper with a tendency to awaken easily.	☐ I am a moderately sound sleeper and need less than eight hours.	☐ I sleep deeply and am often difficult to awaken.
Body Temperature	☐ My hands and feet are cold. I prefer a warm environment.	☐ I am usually warm and prefer a cooler environment.	☐ I am adaptable to most temperatures but dislike cold.
Outlook	☐ I am lively and enthusiastic by nature and like change.	☐ I am purposeful, intense and like to convince. I enjoy challenges and competition. I like to be in command and have been called a natural leader. Some find me pushy, stubborn or opinionated.	☐ I tend to be easy going, relaxed and accepting.
Dreams	☐ My dreams tend to be active, violent, intense and vivid, like being chased or flying. I often forget my dreams.	☐ My dreams tend to be passionate and colorful. I am often chasing or competing. I typically remember dreams.	☐ My dreams are cool and peaceful. I usually remember details.
Voice	☐ I am talkative and speak quickly. Some would call me a chatterbox. My voice is often hoarse or crackly.	☐ My speech is precise and some would say I have a sharp tongue. I am sarcastic and cutting. My voice is typically intense and clear. I am a good public speaker.	☐ My speech is slow and deliberate. My voice tends to be gentle and melodious.
Lifestyle	☐ I am creative, highly imaginative and mentally quick. I am not typically interested in practical applications. My daily routine is irregular. I am very flexible and can change quickly.	☐ I am practical, a planner and very organized.	☐ I am habitual and once I develop a pattern I can keep it up for a long time.
Memory and Learning	☐ I learn quickly and understand almost immediately, but I forget things quickly.	☐ I have a sharp mind and good powers of concentration.	☐ It can take me a bit longer to learn, but I rarely forget. I have outstanding long-term memory.
Reaction to Stress	☐ I tend to respond to stress with fear, worry and anxiety.	☐ Under stress, I tend to become irritated and angry.	☐ Under stress I tend to withdraw or become depressed.

Temperament	I am excitable, lively, fun and tend to be a bit impulsive. I have high energy, usually in short bursts and am full of joy and enthusiasm although my mood is changeable. I tend to tire or over-exert easily. □	I am orderly, self-confident, competitive, assertive, focused and entrepreneurial. I enjoy a challenge but I can be aggressive, demanding and pushy at times. □	I am slow to anger, strive to maintain harmony and peace. I tend to be tolerant, calm, forgiving and loving however, I can exhibit traits of greed, envy, attachment and possessiveness. □
Total for	Vata	Pitta	Kapha

Part I

Part II

The second part of the questionnaire determines imbalances or Vikriti. Mark your answer to each of the following questions. Answer according to what is most true of you now or over the past few months. Score your answers by using the scale: "Never" is 1 point, "Occasionally" is 3 points, "Always" is 5 points.

Vata Assessment

Vata score: Never = 1, Occasionally = 3, Always = 5   Never Occasionally Always

I have been feeling nervous, fearful, panicky, anxious or frantic.

I have been having difficulty falling asleep or have been awakening easily.

I have been acting impulsively or inconsistently.

I have been more forgetful than usual.

I have been feeling restless or uneasy.

My skin is dry and easily chapped.

I am suffering from dry, hard stools, constipation and gas or bloating or I am having loose stools when emotionally upset.

I am becoming intolerant of cold.

My daily schedule of eating meals, going to sleep or waking up has been inconsistent from day to day.

I am having a number of physical concerns including losing weight.

Total Vata score

Pitta Assessment

Pitta score: Never = 1, Occasionally = 3, Always = 5   Never Occasionally Always

I have been feeling irritable or impatient.

I have a red, inflamed or burning rash, acne, cold sores or fever blisters.

I have been feeling critical and intolerant of others.

I enjoy spicy foods but they have been causing heartburn or acid reflux.

I feel like I am overheated or having hot flashes.

My bowels are loose or I am having 2-3 bowel movements a day.

I have been feeling frustrated, irritable or angry.

I have been behaving compulsively and find it difficult to stop once I have started working on a project.

My eyes are red, inflamed or sensitive to light.

I expect perfection of myself and others.

Total Pitta score

Kapha Assessment

Kapha score: Never = 1, Occasionally = 3, Always = 5   Never Occasionally Always

I have excessive mucus in my body, sinuses or lung congestion.

I have been dealing with conflict by withdrawing.

I have been accumulating more clutter than usual in my life.

I am overweight.

I am stubborn and resistant to change.

I am having difficulty leaving a job, a relationship or a situation even though it is not nourishing me.

I have been spending more time watching rather than participating in athletic activity.

It is difficult for me to wake up in the morning even if I sleep deeply for 8 to10 hours.

I am prone to excessive emotional eating especially of sweet, heavy foods.

My bowels movements are slow, sticky and sluggish or feel incomplete.

Total Kapha score

Totals   **Vata Pitta Kapha**

Total for Part I

Total for Part II

Grand Total of Parts I and II

Prakriti: my constitution.
Any number in Part I greater than 10 is your primary constitution.

Vikriti: my current state of balance
If the grand total of Part I and Part II is more than 40, this shows an imbalance.